Positive Stories f[...]
Volum[...]

Six Plays for Young People to Perform in Real Life or Remotely

Tim Crouch, Leyla Josephine, Bryony Kimmings, The PappyShow with Lewis Hetherington, Sara Shaarawi, Robert Softley Gale

Edited by Wonder Fools

methuen | drama

LONDON · NEW YORK · OXFORD · NEW DELHI · SYDNEY

METHUEN DRAMA
Bloomsbury Publishing Plc
50 Bedford Square, London, WC1B 3DP, UK
1385 Broadway, New York, NY 10018, USA
29 Earlsfort Terrace, Dublin 2, Ireland

BLOOMSBURY, METHUEN DRAMA and the Methuen
Drama logo are trademarks of Bloomsbury Publishing Plc

First published in Great Britain 2023

Cover illustrations: Molly Fairhurst

Cover design: Orlando Lloyd

A catalogue record for this book is available from the British Library.

A catalog record for this book is available from the Library of Congress.

ISBN: PB: 978-1-3504-1110-4
ePDF: 978-1-3504-1111-1
eBook: 978-1-3504-1112-8

Series: Plays for Young People

Typeset by Mark Heslington Ltd, Scarborough, North Yorkshire
Printed and bound in Great Britain

To find out more about our authors and books visit
www.bloomsbury.com and sign up for our newsletters.

Positive Stories for Negative Times: Season Three

Six Plays for Young People to Perform
in Real Life or Remotely

Tim Crouch, Leyla Josephine, Bryony Kimmings, The PappyShow
with Lewis Hetherington, Sara Shaarawi, Robert Softley Gale

Edited by Wonder Fools

Positive Stories for Negative Times: Season 3

Produced by Wonder Fools in association with Traverse Theatre,
Ayr Gaiety, Eden Court, Perth Theatre and Youth Theatre Arts
Scotland with plays co-commissioned by Wonder Fools and
Traverse Theatre

Supported by Creative Scotland, the Gannochy Trust, Hugh Fraser
Foundation, William Syson Foundation, Trades Hall of Glasgow
Commonweal Fund and Gordon Fraser Foundation. The Traverse
is supported by Creative Scotland and Edinburgh City Council

Wonder Fools is a Scottish Charity (Registered Number SC047673)

Traverse Theatre (Scotland) is a Limited Company (Registered
Number SC076037) and a Scottish Charity (Registered Number
SC002368) with its Registered Office at 10 Cambridge Street,
Edinburgh, Scotland, EH1 2ED

The Traverse Theatre is funded by Creative Scotland and The City
of Edinburgh Council, with additional support from The Scottish
Government Performing Arts Venues Relief Fund

Positive Stories For Negative Times: Season 3 was first produced by
Wonder Fools from January–July 2023

ABOUT THE PROJECT

SEASON ONE

Positive Stories for Negative Times was born in August 2020 in the midst of the coronavirus pandemic. The innovative and exciting project responded to the lack of physical spaces for young people to participate in creative activities due to the pandemic, and instead allowed them to come together to make new work online or live in the space, if government guidelines allowed.

Wonder Fools commissioned five of the UK's top playwrights to create new work especially for young people to rehearse, explore and perform remotely or in person. Playwrights were Sabrina Mahfouz, Chris Thorpe, Stef Smith, Bea Webster and our very own Robbie Gordon and Jack Nurse.

The project engaged:

2,703 young people

2,000+ audience members

282 groups from 119 organisations, including fifty-seven schools, from across the UK, Spain, Canada and Sweden.

Groups were invited to upload their performances to the Positive Stories website. These can be seen at www.positivestories.scot/season-1/

'A wonderful project providing a platform for young peoples' creativity and engagement at a time when they need it most.'

Suzie Lundy, Teacher, The Royal High School, Edinburgh

SEASON TWO

Positive Stories for Negative Times: Season Two launched in June 2021, after the success of Season One. Season Two grew in both scale and ambition and this included seven brilliant plays of varying styles for groups of any size. As well as being performed, the plays in Season Two were used as a stimulus for all kinds of creative activity.

Wonder Fools and the Traverse Theatre commissioned some of the UK's most exciting voices to write seven new plays for young people. These were developed in collaboration with the Wonder Fools' Youth Board and included not only traditional scripts but also blueprints for devising. Therefore, regardless of a group's size, age, experience or context, there was something for everyone. The brilliant artists commissioned as part of Season Two were Bryony Kimmings, Hannah Lavery, Douglas Maxwell, Debris Stevenson, The PappyShow with Lewis Hetherington and Trav Young Writer Ellen Bannerman as well as Wonder Fools' Robbie Gordon and Jack Nurse.

Season Two stats:

2,830 young participants*

182 teachers and practitioners engaged*

171 groups*

89 organisations and schools*

24 online workshops

11 countries, 5 continents

19 new Youth Board members

7 new plays commissioned

5,000 audience members (approximately)

*These are the numbers of official sign ups to the project. We have since heard of hundreds more young people who have taken part in the project via friends.

Groups were invited to upload their work to the Positive Stories website. These can be seen at www.positivestories. scot/season-2/

'This project has had a real impact on the kind of group we are, the group dynamic, the way we interact with each other, the way we think about making theatre, it's really positively helped.'

Lee, Perfect Circle Youth Theatre, Malvern

SEASON THREE

Positive Stories for Negative Times: Season Three is an international participatory project offering organisations who work with young people a process, newly commissioned plays and training by the best theatre artists working in the UK free of charge. It is produced by Wonder Fools in association with Traverse Theatre, Ayr Gaiety, Eden Court, Perth Theatre and Youth Theatre Arts Scotland with plays co-commissioned by Wonder Fools and Traverse Theatre.

This season, we are taking Positive Stories out on the road and want to get more young people involved than ever before! We have two pathways you can take, like previous seasons, participants can get involved and create anything they like with their chosen play or process. Or for the first time ever, groups have the opportunity to perform at a Positive Stories Festival at one of our four new regional hubs across Scotland in Summer 2023, these are Eden Court (Inverness), Traverse Theatre (Edinburgh), Ayr Gaiety (Ayr) and Perth Theatre (Perth).

Festival dates are:

Traverse Theatre, Edinburgh: 24 and 25 June

The Gaiety, Ayr: 1 and 2 July

Eden Court, Inverness: 8 and 9 July

Perth Theatre, Perth: 15 and 16 July

If you are reading this before 26 May 2023, you can still sign up to take part in the online element of the project – go to www.positivestories.scot to find out more.

PARTICIPANTS OF THE POSITIVE STORIES FESTIVALS 2023

TRAVERSE THEATRE, EDINBURGH – 24 & 25 JUNE

Beath High School

Miss Hanson	Grace
Mrs Watson	Holly
Mr Forbes	Iona
Acid	Kirsty
Aimee	Leigh
Aivah	Mirren
Alex A	Moxxie
Alex B	Olivia
Alfie	Paris
Amanda	Pati
Amy	Ray
Benji	Rosie
Bethany	Roxy
Brooke	Sophie
Caitlin	Tyler
Cara	Yaroslav
Eilish	Zoriana
Emily	

Firhill High School

Lyceum Youth Theatre Minis (8–10)
Director: Heather Johns
Director: Sophie Howell
Assistant Director: Leila Price
Assistant Director: Katy Bancroft
Creative Learning Assistant Producer: Connel Burnett
Creative Learning Producer: Kerrie Walker
Director of Creative Learning: Sharon May

Ada	Anna
Aelle	Annamaria
Alena	Ayanda
Amber	Bella

Carlos
Catherine
Daisy
Eilish
Elizabeth
Ellie
Estelle
Eva
Finlay
Henry
Isabel
Iselle
Ivy
Lila

Lizzie
Nathan
Niamh
Olivia
Rebecca
Robbie
Sienna
Sofia
Solomon
Toby
Tyler
Willow
Yaana

The Mill Youth Theatre (S1 group North Berwick)
Amber
Carmen
Daisy
Daniel
Eve
Isla

Josh
Maia
Murray
Poppy
Rowan
Sophie

Wester Hailes High School Drama Club

THE GAIETY, AYR – 1 & 2 JULY

Drama Llama Youth Theatre

Gaiety Young Company
Group leaders: Steven Leach & Mhairi Gilmour
Aiden
Andrew
Erin
Heidi
Hilary
Holly
Isababella
Katie D

Katie W
Lyla
Maisie
Neve
Philip
Raiona
Tilda
Tyler

Toonspeak
Toonspeak Theatre Makers Juniors
Toonspeak Theatre Makers Intermediate
Toonspeak Theatre Makers Seniors

What Happens Now?

Wonder Fools Youth Board

Arron	Leo
Catriona	Morna
Danny	Sophie
Eve	Vicky

EDEN COURT, INVERNESS – 8 & 9 JULY

Charleston Academy

Eden Court Youth Theatre (11–13s)

Eden Court Collective

Borealis Theatre Arts – Nairn Youth Theatre

PERTH THEATRE, PERTH – 15 & 16 JULY

FADs

Ellie	Luisa
Emma	Megan
Evie	Naomi
George	Tate
Hannah	Thomas
Isla	Zosia
Katrina	

Firefly Arts

Alice	Kennedy
Charlotte	Lily
Emily	Niamh
Esther	Oscar
Kayleigh	Viktoria

Perth Youth Theatre

EDITORS' NOTE

We are delighted to return with a third season of Positive Stories for Negative Times. It is still humbling to us that in the first lockdown in 2020 we initially set out to work with seventy-five groups and now thousands of young people from across the world have participated in the project. We are always bowled over by the creativity and joy of everyone involved and can't wait to see what comes from this new programme of plays.

It's a pleasure to welcome some of our favourite artists to write plays for Season Three – Tim Crouch, Leyla Josephine, Sara Shaarawi and Robert Softley Gale. The work this year is incredibly rich and full of theatrical potential for groups to play with, we can't thank the participating artists enough. We are also really pleased to include the two devising guides from Season Two – Bryony Kimming's *Revolting* and The PappyShow with Lewis Hetherington's *Thanks for Nothing* – giving groups a broad scope of forms and themes to choose from.

The major development of this year's project is the creation of four regional hubs in Scotland, working with the Traverse Theatre, Perth Theatre, Ayr Gaiety and Inverness' Eden Court to host four Positive Stories festivals where local groups can come and perform. It's going to be an amazing series of weekends where young people can connect with different groups and watch each other's work.

We'd like to express our thanks to a range of different people without whom the project could not thrive – the commissioned artists whose work is going to be an inspiration for so many; the Positive Stories team, the wonderful Participation Associates Gemma Nicol and Lisa Williamson who are the point of contact for all participating groups; Serden Salih, our brilliant Marketing and Comms Manager; the ridiculously talented Positive Stories Youth Board who collaborate with the commissioned artists at every step of the creative process to inform the making of the work; the Traverse Theatre who have been invaluable partners with us since Season One; the other festival partners this year Perth Theatre, Ayr Gaiety and Eden Court who we can't wait to visit in the summer; Orlando Lloyd and Neil Scott for making the project look fabulous; and the Wonder Fools Board of Trustees whose support and guidance in steering the company is as vital as ever.

Finally, we'd like to thank every participating young person and group leader past and present for being the lifeblood of the project and filling us with joy every day. We can't wait to see what comes from this year and look forward to seeing you at the Positive Stories Festivals.

Steph, Jack, Robbie
Wonder Fools
April 2023

WONDER FOOLS

ABOUT WONDER FOOLS

'One of the most vibrant young companies to emerge onto to the Scottish theatre scene in recent years'
The Scotsman, 2021

Wonder Fools SCIO (SC047673) is a registered charity and theatre company. We tell untold stories that need to be heard throughout Scotland and beyond. We create exceptional arts experiences relevant to the communities we work with. Our belief is that theatre is for everyone. We work with young people and communities, on stage and off, as collaborators, participants and audience members to ensure their stories are heard and their potential is realised.

Established in 2017, our work takes many forms, shapes, and sizes; whichever is most suited to the stories we are telling. Since March 2020 alone we have produced five digital projects including audio plays, short films, interactive installations and an international participatory project, as well as touring productions performed in rural town halls and on Scotland's most famous stages reaching over 58,000 people in sixteen countries across five continents. All our work is made with the communities in which we perform ensuring that it is relevant, authentic and accessible to them, whilst amplifying their voices through telling their stories to new audiences.

We believe in young people and all our work comes with accompanying creative learning packages to engage new audiences and empowers them to tell their stories too. We offer career development opportunities to young people from across Scotland including paid apprenticeships, workshops and have a youth board made up of twenty young people who guide our work from idea to final performance.

'I am just so continuously impressed by the heart and values at the core of Wonder Fools, everyone who is a part of WF or works with you has been so lovely, every production and project seems to hang on questions of story and accessibility, and I can't think of a single other company whose name is so synonymous with fun and hope. I am so proud to have worked on this show and I am so excited to see what's to come. No one else is doing theatre like you guys and the impact you have in people's lives is huge. Just, thank you.' Sophie, Wonder Fools Youth Board Member

Website: www.wonderfools.org
Twitter: @wonder_fools
Facebook: @wonderfoolsonline
Instagram: @wonder_fools_online

For more information about the company and how you can work support our work please contact

contact@wonderfools.org

WONDER FOOLS TEAM

Robbie Gordon: Co-Founder & Artistic Director
Jack Nurse: Co-Founder & Artistic Director
Steph Connell: Executive Producer
Gemma Nicol (hidden route): Participation Associate
Lisa Williamson (hidden route): Participation Associate
Emma Ruse: Participation Associate
Serden Salih: Marketing Manager

WONDER FOOLS YOUTH BOARD

Molly Bryson
Eve Campbell
Eve Dickson Batchelor
Arron Greechan
Ava Hickey
Catriona Hill

ABOUT THE TRAVERSE

We are the Traverse – champion of stories and storytellers. The stories we share are by anyone and for everyone.

As Scotland's new writing theatre, the Traverse Theatre is a dynamic centre for performance, experience and discovery, enabling people across society to access and engage with theatre is our fundamental mission.

Our year-round programme bursts with new stories and live performances that challenge, inform and entertain. We empower artists and audiences to make sense of the world today, providing a safe space to question, learn, empathise and – crucially – encounter different people and experiences. Conversation and the coming together of groups are central to a democratic society, and we champion equal expression and understanding.

We commission, produce and programme for existing and future audiences to offer new and exciting experiences for everyone, and our partnerships with other theatre companies and festivals enable us to present a wide range of innovative performances.

The Traverse would not exist without our over-arching passion for talent development and embracing the unexplored. We work with the newest and rawest talent – with an emphasis on the Scottish-based – nurturing it to become the art, artists and performances that can be seen on our stages through a variety of creative learning and literary programmes.

The timely, powerful stories that start life on our stages have a global impact, resulting in dozens of tours, productions and translations. We are critically acclaimed and recognised the world over for our originality and artistic risk, which we hope will create some of the most talked-about plays, productions, directors, writers and actors for years to come.

Find out more about the Traverse:

www.traverse.co.uk

With thanks

The Traverse extends grateful thanks to all of its supporters, including those who prefer to remain anonymous. Their valuable contributions ensure that the Traverse continues to champion stories and storytellers in all of its forms, help develop the next generation of creative talent and lead vital projects in our local community, Scotland and beyond.

With your help, we can write the next scene of our story. Visit traverse.co.uk/support-us to find out more.

Traverse Theatre Supporters
DIAMOND
Alan & Penny Barr
Katie Bradford
Kirsten Lamb
David Rodgers

PLATINUM
Judy & Steve
Angus McLeod
Iain Millar
Mike & Carol Ramsay

GOLD
Roger & Angela Allen
Carola Bronte-Stewart
Iona Hamilton

SILVER
Bridget M Stevens
Allan Wilson
Gaby Thomson
Chris & Susan Gifford
Lesley Preston
John Healy

BRONZE
Barbara Cartwright
Alex Oliver & Duncan Stephen

Zakia Moulaoui Guery
Dave Moutrey
Rebecca O'Brien
Donna Reynolds
Bryony Shanahan
May Sumbwanyambe
Christopher Wynn

CREATIVE TEAM

Steph Connell – Executive Producer

Steph is a freelance producer working in theatre and events across the UK. Her experience includes live theatre, digital and outdoor work across new writing, circus, dance and children's theatre.

She is Executive Producer for recently producing flagship participation programme Positive Stories for Negative Times, *549: Scots of the Spanish Civil War* (national tour); *And Then Come the Nightjars* and *Lampedusa* (Citizens Theatre). She is also Producer of Manchester based company ThickSkin for which credits include *Shade*, *Petrichor*, *How Not To Drown*, *Chalk Farm* and as Assistant Producer for The Static. She has recently worked as Associate Producer for Raw Material and is currently Producer for Sleeping Warrior Theatre Company.

Steph was Stage One Producer at the Citizens Theatre in 2017. Other producing credits include *No Way Back* (Frantic Assembly); *Surreal Carnival Experience* (Frantic Assembly/ Underworld); *Leaper – A Fish Tale* and *Finding Victoria* (Tucked In); *Full Stop* and *Playground Victories* (Light The Fuse/Scribbled Thought) and *Superhero Snail Boy* (Scribbled Thought).

Steph has also worked for Tron Theatre, Artichoke, National Theatre of Scotland, Greenwich and Docklands International Festival and National Centre for Circus Arts. She has an MA in Arts and Cultural Management from Queen Margaret University and is a graduate of the Clore Emerging Leaders Course in 2017.

stephconnell.co.uk

Robbie Gordon – Co-Artistic Director

Robbie Gordon is a theatre-maker born in Prestonpans specialising in making work with and for communities. He trained at the Royal Conservatoire of Scotland graduating in 2016. He is the Co-Artistic Director of Wonder Fools and the Creative Engagement Director at the Traverse Theatre.

For Wonder Fools: Co-creator of Positive Stories for Negative Times (Wonder Fools in association with the Traverse Theatre); Writer and Movement Director of *549: Scots of the Spanish Civil War* (Wonder Fools in association with the Citizens Theatre); Writer and Movement Director of *The Coolidge Effect* (Wonder Fools); Writer and Director of *McNeill of Tranent: Fastest Man in the World* (Wonder Fools): Associate Director of *Meet Jan Black* (Ayr Gaiety in association with Wonder Fools); Associate Director of *Lampedusa* (Citizens Theatre in association with Wonder Fools).

Creative Engagement work: Creative Engagement Director of Ayr Gaiety's Culture Collective projects with Jack Nurse; Producer and Director of *Class Act* (Traverse Theatre); Co-creator of the New Scottish Companies Programme (Ayr Gaiety); Speaker at the 2022 Edinburgh International Culture Summit at the Scottish Parliament; Creator of *Open Your Lugs* (Ayr Gaiety); lead artist (Ayrshire) on Danny Boyle's *Pages of the Sea* (National Theatre of Scotland and 1418 NOW); Assistant on Jeremy Deller's *we're here because we're here* (National Theatre of Scotland and 1418 NOW).

Other selected theatre work: Writer of *When the Sun Meets the Sky* (Traverse Theatre and Capital Theatres); Co-movement Director of *The Enemy* (National Theatre of Scotland); Movement Director of Eve Nicol's *Svengali* (Pleasance Theatre in association with Pitlochry Festival Theatre); Associate Director of *Square Go* (Francesca Moody Productions); Movement Director of the *Lost Elves* (Citizens Theatre in association with the Royal Conservatoire of Scotland); Assistant Director for *Julius Caesar* (Company of Wolves); Assistant Director on Graham McLaren's *Dream On!*

(Royal Conservatoire of Scotland and BBC Symphony Orchestra) and Research Assistant on *Locker Room Talk* (Traverse Theatre).

Jack Nurse – Co-Artistic Director

Jack is a director and theatre-maker. He co-founded Glasgow-based theatre company Wonder Fools in 2014. Recently, Jack was an Origins Artist with Headlong (2021–2), and Co-Creative Engagement Director at the Ayr Gaiety.

Currently: Directing *24 (Day)* by Annie Jenkins for the Almeida Theatre in association with All Change, Arsenal in the Community and Cardboard Citizens; Artist in Residence (Creative Development) at the Traverse Theatre and co-artistic lead of the international participatory project Positive Stories for Negative Times.

Training: Royal Conservatoire of Scotland and the National Theatre Studio Directors' Course.

As Director/Writer: *549: Scots of the Spanish Civil War*, *The Coolidge Effect* (Wonder Fools); *When the Sun Meets the Sky* (Traverse Theatre/Capital Theatres).

As Director: *And Then Come the Nightjars* (Wonder Fools); *Lampedusa* (Citizens Theatre/Wonder Fools); *Meet Jan Black* (Wonder Fools/Ayr Gaiety); *The Essence of the Job is Speed* (Almeida Theatre); *Larchview* (National Theatre of Scotland/ BBC Scotland); *The Lost Elves* (Citizens Theatre/RCS); *The Mack, The Storm* (Play, Pie, Pint/Traverse Theatre).

As Associate/Assistant Director: *Red Dust Road* (National Theatre of Scotland/HOME); *The Broons* (Sell A Door); *Dr Dolittle* (Music & Lyrics); *Oresteia: This Restless House* (Citizens Theatre/National Theatre of Scotland); *Blackbird* (Citizens Theatre); *The Winter's Tale* (Royal Lyceum); *Hay Fever* (Royal Lyceum/Citizens Theatre).

www.jacknurse.com

Serden Salih – Marketing Manager

Serden Salih is a freelance marketing manager, events coordinator and film historian/artist, with 10+ years experience in both the film industry and creative arts sector. He graduated with an MA in Film, Television and Screen Media from Birkbeck, University of London in 2015 and went on to work as a distribution manager handling press/marketing for one of the UK's most recognised LGBT film distributors, Peccadillo Pictures. Serden has also worked at various festivals across the UK and internationally, including the Berlin International Film Festival, BFI London Film Festival, Edinburgh Festival Fringe and the Edinburgh Film Festival. He also has a background in film production and programming.

In 2015, Serden worked as a second Assistant Director and played a small role in the infamous short film *Trouser Bar* which premiered at the BFI Flare: London LGBT+ Film Festival in 2016 and went on to appear at film festivals worldwide including NYC, Helsinki, Brussels, Buenos Aires, Torino, Madrid and Berlin. The film won 'Best International Short Film' at *MixBrasil* film festival in São Paulo. Furthermore, he helped win the Screen Award for 'Specialist Film Campaign of the Year' for Ciro Guerra's *Embrace of the Serpent* and achieved the highest grossing film for Peccadillo Pictures at the time.

He is the Marketing Manager for Glasgow based Wonder Fools who has marketed the flagship participation programme *Positive Stories for Negative Times* as well as previous productions of *And Then Come The Nightjars* and *549: Scots of the Spanish Civil War* (2022 national tour). He has also worked for ThickSkin Theatre on *Blood Harmony* and is currently a Digital Content Associate at the Traverse Theatre and Communications Manager for Scotland based film programmer, CinemaAttic.

Gemma Nicol and Lisa Williamson – Participation Associates

Gemma Nicol and Lisa Williamson are co-artistic directors of hidden route theatre company, lecturers in Acting and Performance at Dundee and Angus College and the Positive Stories for Negative Times Participation Associates.

Collectively they have been working within the participatory arts sector for over twenty-five years, collaborating with communities and organisations such as Stellar Quines, V&A Dundee, Youth Theatre Arts Scotland, National Theatre of Scotland, Dundee Rep Theatre, macrobert, Perth Theatre, The Point and AMATEO.

Gemma and Lisa love to create work that is driven by collaboration and curiosity, and are passionate about creating opportunities to creatively explore non-traditional theatre spaces. Fundamentally, the work they make is about amplifying the voices and creative potential of the young people they work with.

www.hiddenroute.co.uk

ARTISTS

Leyla Josephine

Award-winning filmmaker, playwright, poet and creative writing facilitator Leyla Josephine was named one of Screen International's Rising Stars Scotland 2022. She recently took part in Edinburgh International Film Festival Talent Lab and is a BAFTA Connect member.

Her solo shows *Hopeless* and *Daddy Drag* have taken the UK by storm with sold out shows across the country. She has also been featured on BBC Radio 4, BBC The Social, The Guardian Online, Buzzfeed, Huffington Post, Upworthy, The National and The Scotsman and Choice Words: Writers on Abortions alongside the likes of Margaret Atwood, Audre Lorde and Gloria Steinem.

www.leylajosephine.co.uk

Bryony Kimmings

Bryony Kimmings is a playwright, performer, documentary maker and screen writer from the UK. She is inspired by female stories, social taboos and dismantling power structures. Kimmings' work is brutally honest, very funny and often a bit geeky and dangerous.

Bryony's stage work includes her plays (as writer and performer): *Sex Idiot, 7 Day Drunk, Credible Likeable Superstar Role Model, Fake It 'Til You Make It* and *I'm a Phoenix, Bitch*.

Her TV and film work includes the documentaries *The Sex Clinic* (C4) and *Opera Mums* (BBC) and the feature film *Last Christmas*, which Bryony cowrote with Emma Thompson.

www.bryonykimmings.com

The PappyShow with Lewis Hetherington

Thanks For Nothing is a collaboration between The PappyShow and playwright Lewis Hetherington.

The PappyShow is a playful and physical ensemble theatre company who create distinctive and critically acclaimed productions, lead inclusive workshops rooted in kindness, and work tirelessly to develop the industry we move in through connection and uplifting. The PappyShow was formed in 2013 by Kane Husbands to bring people together to move, dance, create moments of radical joy, share stories and take time just to PLAY!

Productions *BOYS* and *GIRLS* were critically acclaimed for their vibrant, revelatory and expectation-defying explorations of contemporary masculinity and femininity. Our upcoming shows *What Do You See* and *Black Girl Magic* will delve even deeper into exploring and elevating the underrepresented identities that we want to see on stage.

www.thepappyshow.co.uk

Lewis Hetherington is an award-winning playwright, director and performance maker. His work is rooted in collaboration and storytelling. He is passionate about the arts creating space for social change. He has won two Fringe First Awards, the Arches Brick Award, and an Adelaide Fringe Award. He is one of the co-directors of fieldwork performance. His work has toured extensively throughout Scotland and the rest of the world including performances in Australia, Canada, China, Germany, Japan, Saudi Arabia, Singapore and the USA.

Tim Crouch

Tim is a playwright, director, performer and theatre maker based in Brighton, UK. He was an actor before he started to write and he still performs in much of his work.

Tim's plays are characterised by an attention to their audience. There is a devotion to the liveness of theatre and a recognition that the audience are the ultimate collaborators in the creation of meaning at the point of performance. The plays are meticulously scripted but engineered in such a way to ensure that no two performances are identical. From the inanimate objects donated by the audience in *My Arm*, to the unrehearsed second actor in *An Oak Tree*, to the audience writing in *I, Cinna (the poet)* and their reading in *Total Immediate Collective Imminent Terrestrial Salvation*, to the audience embodying otherness in *ENGLAND* and *Truth's a Dog Must to Kennel*. Tim's plays are narratively driven but pay as much attention to their form as to their story.

www.timcrouchtheatre.co.uk

Sara Shaarawi

Sara Shaarawi is a playwright from Cairo, based in Glasgow. In 2017, Sara began to take on producing projects, most notably project managing the Arab Arts Focus showcase at the Edinburgh Fringe Festival and partnering with the Workers Theatre to crowdfund and create Megaphone, a new bursary aimed at supporting artists of colour based in Scotland.

In 2021, Sara's first play, *Niqabi Ninja*, was produced by Independent Arts Project (Edinburgh) in association with Hewar Company (Alexandria); it opened at Shubbak Festival in London, followed by a Scotland-wide tour and a run at the Edinburgh International Festival.

Sara is also an occasional performer, performing in rehersed readings and often comperes events in Scotland, such as *Chill Habibi* and *Morning Manifesto*.

www.sarashaarawi.com

Robert Softley Gale

Robert is the Artistic Director of Birds of Paradise (BOP), Scotland's touring theatre company that promotes the work of disabled artists in partnership with non-disabled artists and mainstream theatre venues and companies. Robert sits on the board of the National Theatre of Scotland and his previous work with the company includes *My Left/Right Foot the Musical* (Birds of Paradise); *Girl X* (Traverse Theatre, Citizens Theatre, Dundee Rep Theatre, Eden Court Theatre). Other theatre works include *If These Spasms Could Speak* (Arches, toured to Brazil, Estonia, Ireland, India and USA); *Wendy Hoose* (Birds of Paradise); *Purposeless Movements* (nominated for CATS Best Director award).

www.softley.co.uk

Are You A Robot?
by Tim Crouch

Description

Two groups of children meet. They look the same; they imagine similar things; they make almost the same noises; they dance in almost the same way. But one group is a digital version of the other; they are the face we see reflected back to us online; they're exciting and demanding and hard to live up to. The two groups try to work each other out and decide if they can exist together.

This is a joyful collision between real and fake, perfect and imperfect, human and robot.

It's an investigation into – and a celebration of – humanness.

The cast can be as big as you like.

This play could be in the round. It doesn't have to be in a theatre. It could be in a school hall or a community centre or any space.

Writer's Note

This is a playful play. Enjoy using all the space you have available – from the back of the audience/auditorium to inside the audience and all over the stage!

Rhythm is very important in this play – it's like a piece of music with different tempos. Some bits can zip along with no spaces between the lines. See how fast you can go! Some bits are worked out slowly. There are nice spaces and stops and starts. The stage directions help you to explore this. Also, where there are spaces between the lines, you can take your time. Where there are no spaces, get a move on! Enjoy rehearsing the rhythms.

I think it's important that the young actors don't pretend to be anyone other than themselves. The actors are not playing individual 'characters'. The lines spoken by the **Human***s represent one idea of humanness. The lines spoken by the* **Not***s represent one idea of digital humanness. Two collective voices played by as many young people as you like. For example, on page 31:*

Human   I love my old unicorn sweatshirt that still smells of my dog. 🐾

Human   It's too small for me now. 😖

Human   I wish I could stop growing. 😔

Human   That shirt! 😩

Four different voices. Each talking about their relationship to their own sweat shirt. Each also talking about the idea of one sweat shirt that belongs to them all. It's the same thing with references to ears and eyes, etc. on pages 6–8. It's your own ear but it's also everyone's ear!

The actors playing **Not**s *should not appear like robots. They are very convincing humans! They're almost impossible to distinguish from* **Human**s. *Just a little smarter, a little neater, more polished. A little better at things. It's what they say that makes us question their humanness. Also, the* **Not**s *can't enter the audience space. They are not one of us. They are not 'from' us. At the end, they are left on the stage when the* **Human**s *and the audience leave the theatre.*

The emojis are there to help the actors think about the energy behind the lines. For example, the word 'yeah' can be said in many ways. Like 😀 or 😑 or 😏 etc. Sometimes, emojis exist with no word or line attached. This is an indication of the energy in the space between words. A 😶 space is very different to a 😊 space. Have fun with this. Some of the **Not**s' *emojis become really weird and abstract towards the end. Above all, the emojis are playful indicators of performance. You might find better ones – and you would be welcome to!*

The lines can be divided any way you like. At the beginning I've put a 1, 2 and 3 – just to be clear who starts the speaking. After this, you can give lines however you want. Working out who speaks is also part of the rehearsal.

Have fun!

The Play

First actor enters from the audience and walks onto the performance area. They are alone. They take a moment. (Take lots of moments!)

1   Alexa. 🤚

A moment.

1   Hey, Alexa. 👋

Another moment.

1   Alexa. Show me a human. 👣

*Second actor enters from the audience and walks onto the performance area. There are now two actors. **1** and **2**. Take your time. Enjoy your presence. Enjoy the audience not knowing what's coming next!*

A moment.

1 *(presenting the second actor to the audience)*   💗 A human! 😵

2   That's me! 😀 Look. 😃

The second actor does something human – like a little wiggle, maybe. Something fun. You decide. 👋

👣👣👣

A moment.

Second actor speaks:

2   Okay Google. 🤚

A moment.

2   Google. ☝

Another moment.

2   Hey, Google! 👋 Show me a human. 👣

A third actor enters from the audience and walks onto the performance area.

A moment.

1 (*presenting the third actor*)   Good human. 😄

2 (*presenting the third actor*)   Kind human. 😌

3   Nervous human. 😵😵😵

A moment.

Third actor speaks:

3   Hey, Siri. ✋

A moment.

3   SIRI. 😠 Stupid Siri. 😡

Another moment.

3   Siri, show me some humans. 👉

A chair is presented on the performance area.

1   No, Siri! 😶

Another object on the performance area – maybe a fire extinguisher 🧯 or even a dog is brought on 🐕 Make it a game! What are the least human things?

2   No way, Siri! 😳

Another object – maybe a pot of hummus.

1, **2** *and* **3** (*together*)   No, Siri, not hummus, Humans! 😤

A number of actors make themselves known – in the audience. They introduce themselves with the lines below – one by one. (Remember that the emojis give an idea of the energy of the line.) Some **Human***s come onto the stage. Some stay with the audience. They inhabit the whole room. The lines are now divided any way you like – between the whole company.*

Human. 😐

Human. 😐

All too human! 😩

Definitely human. 😑

The last time I looked . . . human! 🙂

I'd say: human! 😶

Etc.

*All the **Human**s introduce their 'humanness'. Everyone gets to say a version of 'I am human'. You can decide.*

Half the company is now present – in the audience and on the performance area.

They are loose and alive and alert and playful and friendly and they fill the spaces in the room.

They are lovely humans. 💜

A moment.

Look, everyone:

All (*loud!*)   HUMANS! 👏👏👏

The audience is invited to clap, maybe!

👏

👏

👏

A moment.

This voice – the voice speaking this now – is the sound of a human outside. 🗣

Being heard by a human inside. 👂

Speaking and hearing. 🗣👂

Inside and outside. 🙂🙂

Front to back. 🙂🙂

Top to toe. 🔝👣

Human. 😑

How about a dance?

Soon.

Everyone can refer to their own voice, ear, eye, etc when they speak. They all add up to the idea of ONE voice, ear, eye, etc.

This ear – this one here – is a human ear.

The bones in this ear are human.

Tiny bones.

Teeny tiny human bones.

This voice – this one now – making the tiny bones in this ear – (*Another actor's ear.*)

vibrate is a human thing.

The wax in this ear is also human.

Waxy waxy!

Some ears don't hear so well and that too is also completely human.

The space between this voice . . .

. . . and this ear (*As far away from the voice as possible.*)

. . . is human.

(*Whispered.*) Even when it's very quiet.

(*Shouted.*) Or very loud.

This is a human voice.

It can do these things:

A joyful, deafening, sloppy, chaotic chorus of sounds, songs, calls, trills, arpeggios, yodelling, etc. from everyone.

Ends in laughter and high fives.

Applause from the audience.

A moment.

This me is human. 😖

And me here. 😃

100 per cent human. 💯

110 per cent. 😊

Is there 110 per cent?

There's anything. 🦇

Really? 🤭

If you can think it – 😊

you can have it! 😇

Says who? 🤓

Humans! 😋

150 per cent! 🎉

700 per cent! 💩

This eye is human. 👁

Blue eye. 👁

Brown eye. 👁

Green eye. 👁

Human eye. 👁

The space between this eye . . .

. . . and this human over here

➡➡➡

. . . is human.

Between this eye . . .

➡➡➡

. . . and the back of this room (*One of the* **Human**s *is at the back of the room.*)

➡➡➡

. . . is human.

Some eyes don't see so well and that too is also completely human. 🦙

Hey, Siri, show me a human space. 🏠😎

This is. 👆

Human space. 🏠😊

This is a human space. 🏠😊

All over here is human space. 🏠😊

And here. (*The ceiling.*) 🏠😊

Here. (*The walls.*) 🏠😊

And over there. 🏠😊

➡➡➡

And all where you (*the audience*) are is, too. 😊

You're human, too, audience. 😊

You're one of us. 😊

You're perfect! 😊

Eleven out of ten! 11😊

All this is human. 👌

This calls for a dance! 🕺

Soon. ⏲

😶

Humans can do this. 😆 (*An inexpert cartwheel or a rubbish handstand or something.*)

I'm good at this sort of thing. 😬 (*A pretty poor attempt at patting head and rubbing tummy at the same time or something.*)

I practised this and look. 😋 (*An inexpert roly-poly or a rubbish crab or something.*)

All actions are accompanied by joy and laughter.

And applause from the audience.

Humans are great. 😎

We are perfect humans. 😍

All humans are perfect. 😊

Humans can imagine things, too. 🤔

Imagine! 😛

Imagine imagining things. 🤓

Imagining easy things. 🖐

Imagining hard things. 😵

(*Inexpertly.*) Can you imagine an imaginary menagerie manager imagining managing an imaginary menagerie. 🖌

😳

Applause.

👏

👏

👏

*A **Human** picks up the chair.*

This chair can be anything. 💪

Whatever we want. 👍

An elephant. 🐘

Yes! 👌

The chair becomes all these things. You can add some more of your own if you want. Find ones that work for you. Please add some more of your own! Make it a game. Find things in rehearsal and add them! These are just suggestions. You could also ask the audience to get involved in this game at this moment in the show – what else could the chair be, audience?! Play!

A bike. 🚲

Yes. 👌

A dragon. 🐉

Definitely. 👍

Jumbo jet. ✈️

Why not? 👌

A crown. 👑

Absolutely. 👌

A monkey. 🐒

Have a banana. 👌

A medal. 🏅

Medal for you! 👍

A castle. 🏰

Attack! 👌

A polar bear. 🐻‍❄️

Save the planet! 👌

Covid. 🦠

The chair is put down quickly!

Run away!

Everyone runs away from the chair!

And also, if we imagine it, it can also be a human.

What?

A human chair!

(They have a conversation with the chair: 'Hi, chair, how are you doing?' 'I'm doing fine, thanks, everyone.' 'What you been up to?' 'Oh, you know, just sitting around, really.' 'I'm thinking about getting my legs waxed.' Think of funny things a chair would say. Etc.)

In this space anything can be anything we want it to be!

This is by the seaside.

This is in the cold sea.

Here comes a wave.

Look out.

Swim, everyone!

(They all run and 'swim'.)

You can find some other things the space can be. These are just suggestions.

This is my nan's flat.

Nice.

I'm my nan.

I'm my nan's nan.

I'm my nan's nan's nan.

You're so old!

Watching you from history.

I've got my eye on you. 👀

'You being a good great great great great grandchild?' 🌀

Yes, great great great great nan. 🏅

'I'm history.' 🌀

I love you, Nan. 🖤

I'm a cloud. ☁️

I'm a cloud raining on you all. 🌧️

Argh! 🎋

I'm rain. 💦

I'm wet. 💦

Wet! 💦

Wet! 💦

They run to find 'shelter'. 🏃 🏃 🏃 🛖

Fill the space! It's a game!

I'm a hot air balloon floating above you, cloud. 🎈

I'm a bird above you, balloon. 🐦

I'm a rocket above you, bird. 🚀

This is on a space station. 🛰️

I'm an astronaut. 👨‍🚀

I'm an astronaut doing a spacewalk. 🎆

(They all spacewalk. Play!) No gravity! 👨‍🚀

Wow. 😮

Okay. 👍

Okay. 👍

👍

A moment.

Now we dance? 🪃

A pause.

Now we dance! 🏃

Big music plays.

The **Human***s all run onto the performance area.*

They dance – free and joyful.

As they dance, they are joined by the other half of the cast (the **Not***s). They come from off-stage/backstage and they dance with the* **Human***s. Initially, the two dancing groups mingle but then they gradually separate. The* **Not***s are neater than the* **Human***s, hair in place, shoes cleaner, etc. They dance differently. If you looked closely at them you would see that they have less joy.*

The **Human***s can (and do) go into the audience. The* **Not***s stay on the performance area.*

The dance stops. The two groups face each other.

The **Not***s are physically still and un-puffed.*

The **Human***s are breathless from their dancing.*

These next five lines can be sort of spoken over each other – all together. Add some more so all the **Human***s can say how puffed they are.*

Human   Ay ay. 😵

Human   Stitch. 😵

Human   Flip. 😵

Human   Oof. 😵

Human   Get my breath back. 😵

They continue to look at each other – suspiciously.

😵

Eventually:

Human   Unexpected item in the bagging area.

*The **Human**s do slowed-down waves/gestures at the **Not**s – don't follow the emojis, make your own gestures/actions – like a mirroring game. The emojis here are about the words more than the movements. The **Not**s mirror the **Human**s' actions, over the following lines:*

Human   Hey. 🙌

Not   Hey. 🙌

Human   Hey. 🙌

Not   Hey. 🙌

Human   Hello. 🙌

Not   Hello. 🙌

Human   Hi. 🙌

Not   Hi. 🙌

Human   We recognise you. ✋

Not   We recognise *you*! 🖐

Human   Look familiar. 🖐

Not   Similiar. 🖐 (*'Similiar' pronounced in a way that rhymes with 'familiar'!*)

Human   Do we know you? ✌

Not   Us? ✌

Human   You. ✋

Not   All of us? 👈

Human   All of you. 🙌

Not   Yes. 👍

Not   Of course you know us. 💭

Not   We know you. 👍

Not   Look. 👋

Human   Who are you? 🙌

Not   We're just some other humans. 🖐

Not   Like you. 🤚

Not   Humans like you. 🖐

Not   Alike you. 💪

Not   Just alike you. 🖐

Not   Just we like you. 👌

Not   We like you very much. 👏

Not   We're your friends. 🤝

Not   We want to be your friends. 🤟

Not   Your best friends. 🤙

Not   Like us. 👍

Not   Please like us. 👆

Not   Like us. 👍

Not   Like. 👍

Not   Like. 👍

Not   Like. 👍

Not   Like. 👍

Not   Like. 👍

Not   Like. 👍

Not (*all*)   LIKE! 👍

🤖 *An awkward moment.* 🤖

Human   Great! 😊

Human   Great?? 😠

Human   Great! 😊

Human   Okay. 😐

Human   Cool humans like us. 😄

Human   Shiny humans like us. 😵

Human   Cool! 😃

😐

Human   Hey. 😑

Human   Hey. 😊

Human   Hey, I love your outfit. 👕

Not   Thanks. 🙏

Not   Everyone's wearing things like this now. 😌

Human   Are they? 😕

Not   Haven't you seen? 😏

Not   Everyone. 😌

Not   Oh, everyone. 😌

Human   I love your hair. 💇

Not   Thanks. 🙏

Not   Everyone has their hair like this now. 🦢

Human   Do they? 😐

Not   Oh, definitely. 😌

Human   I love your skin. 🧴

Not   Thanks. 🙏

Not   Everyone has their skin like this now. 🦢

Human Do they? 😶

Not Didn't you know?

Human Yeah. 😊

Not You can have a discount code! 🖐

Human Right. 😊

Human Hey. ✋

Human Hey, I love your nose. 👃

Not Thanks! 🙏

Not Everyone has their nose like this now. 🖐

Human Do they? 😶

Not Everyone. 🖐

Human Yeah. 😊

Not They do, don't they. 😔

Human Yeah. 😶

Not It's cool being human. 😔

Human Yeah. 😶

Not Humans can do this:

*The **Not**s perform the physical actions done by the **Human**s – but much, much better. An expert handstand, brilliant roly-poly, expert crab, etc. Neither joy nor laughter – just precision and ability.* 🤸🤸‍♂️

*The **Human**s have their noses put out of joint (not literally).* 👃

Not We can make these sounds:

*The **Not**s sing a perfect something a cappella, something modern, harmonies, beat-boxing, you name it.* 🎼🎼🎼

*The **Human**s feel a bit got-at.*

Human Cool. 😊

Not   We can imagine things. 🤓

Not   Imagine. ⊞

Not   Imagine 12 to the power of 10. 😔

Human   Right. 🤖

Not   Imagine sub atomic particles. 😌

Human   Okay. 😃

Not   Imagine infinity. ∞

Human   Um. 😕

Not   Imagine evolution. 🤓

Not   Imagine wifi. 🤓

Not   Black holes. 🤓

Not   Pixels. 🤓

Not   Driverless cars. 🤓

Not   Imagine 01010101 🤓

Human   Lost me. 🍦

A moment.

*The **Human**s don't quite know what's going on.* 😶

Human   Look, this is really nice and everything, but – 😳

Not (*interrupting/backtracking*)   Don't you love it when dogs do cute things. 🐶

Human   Yes! 😄

All this can be really quick, like the lines falling over each other, tumbling out.

Not   On skateboards. 🛹

Human   Oh, yes! 😄

Human   Skateboards! 🛹🛹🛹

Not   Or dogs jumping up and down for something. 🐾 😄

Not   Or dogs watching telly and they think it's real! 😋

Not   Or dogs smelling flowers. 🌷 😄

Human   Yes! 😄

Not   Or when a baby bites your finger. 👶

Human   I love that! 😄

Not   Or babies laughing together. 👯

Human   Yes! 😄

Not   Or a baby plays with a cat! 👯

Human   A kitten! 😄

Not   Or a kitten plays with a baby. 👯 👶

Human   Kittens are so cute! 😄

Not   Or when kids do a funny dance.

Human   Suppose so. 😐

Not   Or there's a funny song. 🎤 😄

Human   Okay. 😐

Not   And crazy food fights. 🍩 😜

Not   Or crazy make-up tips. 💄

Not   And crazy famous people doing crazy things! 💅

Human   Huh. 😳

Not   Or someone gets bumped doing the dumbest thing – 😳 😄

Not   – but not too badly bumped. 👯

Not   Yeah! 😄

Not   Not too badly bumped. 😊

Not   And it's really 👯

Not . . . really 💀

Nots *(all)*   FUNNY!! 😩😵😩💀💀💀

A moment.

Human   Right. 😐

😶

😶

A moment.

An awkward moment.

Not   We can do this: 💃

The **Not**s *all do the floss, maybe – or the latest craze.*

Human   Okay. 😩

Human   We get the picture. 😳

Not   We're your number one best friends forever! 😁

Human   Forever. 😊

Not   And ever. 🎉

Not   Without us, what would you be? 😔

Human   I guess. 🙋

Not   We complete you. 🧍 🧍

Human   So you say. 🙋

Not   It feels good, doesn't it. 👊

Human   Kind of. 🙋

Not   In the same space. 👊

Not   Together in the same place. 👊

Not   It feels good. 👊

Not   You know it feels good. 👊

Not Makes your brain tingle. ✦

Not Makes you come back for more. 👊

Not And more! 👊

Not And more! 👊

Not More. 👊

Not More. 👊

Not More. 👊

Not More. 👊

Not More. 👊

Not More. 👊

A moment.

The **Human***s look at each other. A silent conflab.*

They face the **Not***s.*

Human Would you like to play with us? 😎

Not Sure! 😺

Not What? ☝

Human Tag? 🔷

Not Okay. 💪

Human I'm it. 😊

Nothing happens.

Human Come on! 😊

Nothing happens.

Not Just. ✋

Human What? 😊

Not Just. ✋

Not   One thing. 🤚

Not   Just. 👆

Not   One small thing. 🤏

Human   What? 🤔

Not   Well. 😬

Not   It's like this. 😬

Not   This is the thing. 😬

Not   The thing is. 😬

Not   Have you got any money? 💰

Human   What? 🤔

Not   Money. 💰

Human   Money? 🤔

Not   Money. 💰

Human   Money. 💰

Not   Just a bit. 🤏

Human   Why? 🤔

Not   Just a dollar. 💵

Human   Why? 🤔

A moment.

Not   Money makes the world go round. 😵

Not   That's right. 😵

Not   Round and round and round. 🐎

😵

Human   Only it doesn't, does it. 😶

Not   What? 😐

Human   It doesn't make the world go round. 😳

Human   The world's going round anyway. 🌐

😳

Not   One buck. $

Human   No. 🏠

😳

Human   What's wrong with you? 😳

Not   Nothing! 😄

Not   Nothing! 😄

Human   You sure? 😕

Not   Everything's great! 😄

Not   100 per cent! 😄

Human   110 per cent? 📌

Not   What? 🏃

Human   Is it great 110 per cent? 📌

Not   No. 🤖

Not   Can't be. 🤖

Not   Never. 🤖

Not   No. 🤖

Not   Can't have 110 per cent. 🤖

Not   Oh, no. 🤖

Not   Can't. 🤖

Not   Not possible. 🤖

Not   Per cent actually means out of 100 and so I think you'll find that it's actually not – 😳

Human (*interrupting*)   We'll give you a quid. 📖

Not   A dollar. $

Human   We've only got a quid. £

Not   A dollar. $

Human   A quid. £

Not   A dollar. $

Human   A quid. £

Not   A dollar. $

Human   A quid. £

Not   A rouble? ₽

Human   What? 😵

Not   A rouble. ₽

Human   A rouble? 😵

Not   A rouble. ₽

Not   We'd take a rouble. 👇

Human   What's a rouble? 😵

Human   Russian money. 💴

Human   This is _____ (*The name of the town in which the play is being performed.*)

Not   Use the app, then. 📲

Human   What? 😵

Not   The app. 📱

Human   What app? 😵

Not   The cash app. 📲

Not   The app for the cash. 📱

Not   Slide it over. 😃

Not   Ping it over. 😃

Human   I'm ten. 🤖 (*Or whatever age the actor is.*)

A moment.

Not   We'll take the quid. £

A transaction. A **Human** *gives a* **Not** *one pound.*

Human   Okay now? 🧍

Not   Never better. 🙂

Human   Let's play. 🙂

A game of tag on the stage. Fast and funny at first. Then a bit scary.

The **Human***s encourage the* **Not***s to play among the audience, but they won't.*

The **Not***s introduce shooting into the game – with imagined guns.*

Tag becomes being 'shot'.

The **Not***s line up with imaginary guns and shoot and shoot the* **Human***s.*

Maybe there is the amplified sound of guns and explosions which begins quietly and becomes deafening.

The **Human***s play at first but then become confused and unimpressed.*

The **Human***s refuse to 'die'.*

The **Not***s mime an array of horrible weapons going off – big guns, grenades, rocket launchers, etc – with sound effects.* 🔫 🔫 🔫 🔫

Human   Hey. 😠

Human   Hey! 😧

Human   Hey. 😨

Human   Stop this. 😟

Human   Stop. 😩

Humans (*all*)   STOP!!! 😎

The **Not**s *eventually stop firing. The sound stops.*

Human   This is not what we said. 🐱

Not   You love this. 😎

Human   I was scared. 😟

Not   Wanna have a go with my rocket launcher? 🔫

Human   NO!!!!! ⛔

Human   This is not what we said. 🐾

Human   This isn't playing. 🎯

Human   It's just you shooting us. ☠️

Human   Bullies. 👊

A moment.

Human   Can we have our pound back? 😳

Not   Spent it. 🤭

Human   How? 😕

Not   It went. 😎

Human   Where? 😶

Not   The webpage you're trying to reach cannot be found. 😵

😳

Human   Can we ask you a question? 🐱

Human   Who are you in our space? 🐱🐱

Not   We're just humans like you. 🖐

Human   Prove it. 😕

Not   We look like you. 🖐

Not   We do the same things that you do. 🖐

Not   We love the same things that you love. 🖋

Human   Name them? 😳

Not   Sunsets. 🌄

Human   I suppose so. 😔

Not   And cuddly things. 🧸

Human   Yeah. 🌕

Not   And shiny new stuff. ✨

Human   Maybe. 🌑

Not   And shopping. ⏩

Not   And messaging. ⏩

Not   And stuff about celebrities. ⏩

Not   And buying stuff. ⏩

Not   And taking stuff out of boxes. ⏩

Not   And pretty stuff. ⏩

Not   And boyish boys. ⏩

Not   And girly girls. ⏩

Not   And health spas. ⏩

Not   And skin care. ⏩

Not   And cup cakes. ⏩

Not   And onesies. ⏩

Not   And looking at funny videos. ⏩

Not   And famous people. ⏩

Not   And sleepovers. ⏩

Not   And browsing. ⏩

Not   And money. ⏩

Not   And liking.

Not   And spending money.

Not   And nature things like mountains and

Not   And

Not   And

Not   Trees

Not   Yeah trees

Not   And

Not   All the same stuff.

Not   All the favourites.

Not   Like the favourites.

Not   Favourite likes.

Not   Like.

Not   Like.

Not   Like.

Not   Like.

Not   Like.

Not   Like.

A moment.

Human   Yes, but, you see –

Human   It's like this.

Human   What I love changes all the time.

Human   Me too.

Human   Sometimes I love my brother. 🖤

Human   Sometimes I hate him. 😠

Human   Yes. 👆

Human   Sometimes I love to be tickled. 😄

Human   Sometimes I hate it. 😩

Human   Depends who's doing the tickling. ¿

Human   I used to love chocolate milkshakes but then I had too much and threw up in the car and now even if I think about chocolate milkshakes I feel sick. 🤢

👍👍👍

Human   Sometimes I think the world is beautiful. 😊

Human   Yes. 👆

Human   Sometimes I think the world is dying. 😭

Human   Sometimes I don't know. 😵

Human   Yes. 👆

Human   Yes. 👆

Human   I don't know. 🐦

Human   I want to love everyone, but it's hard. 😔

Human   Some humans are hard to love. 😟

Human   I love my old unicorn sweatshirt that still smells of my dog. 🦄

Human   It's too small for me now. 😫

Human   I wish I could stop growing. 🙈

Human   That shirt! 👕

Not   Buy a new one. 😄

Human   What? 😶

Not   Buy a new one. 😀

Human   You don't understand. 😒

Not   No. *You* don't understand. 😠

😵

Human   I miss my dog. 💔

Human   I want to grow up. ⬆️

Human   Sometimes I do. 😵

Human   Sometimes I think about dying. 🔪

Human   Sometimes I want to stay in bed all day. 🛏️

Human   Sometimes I love school. 😀

Human   Sometimes I hate school. 😡

Human   Sometimes I cry because I can't decide whether I'd rather be sticky all over or hairy all over. 😵

Human   Which is a stupid problem to cry about. 😌

Human   I agree. ☝️

Human   Sometimes I just want to be on my own. 🙈

Human   Sometimes I wish there was no money. ▶️

Human   Sometimes I wish I could win the lottery. 🤑

Human   Sometimes I love myself. ✊

Human   Sometimes I make mistakes. ⚠️

Human   But mostly sort of mostly I'm mostly okay mostly being sort of this. 👍

Human   Human. 😑

Human   Human. 😑

Human   Mostly. 😊

Human   Mostly. 😊

Human   Well? 😊

Nots (*all*)   😊😊😊😊

Human   Well? 😊

The chair.

Human   What's this, then? 😊

Not   A chair. ◼

*Over the following exchanges, the **Human**s slowly move into the audience.*

Human   But what could it be? 😊

Not   A chair? a

Not   It could be a chair. ⊕

Not   A chair. ⊞

Human   I know, but what else? 😊

Not   A chair three-sixty. Ö

Not   One-eighty degrees. ⚥

Not   Ninety degrees. ε

Not   Forty-five degrees. ρ

Not   Total chair. ◎

Not   Wooden chair. ⊞

Not   For sitting on. ♋

Not   For humans to sit on. ⌂

Not   It's a chair. ω

Human   But what else could it be? 😊

Not   A celebrity's chair? 🎴

Not   Money. ⊘

Not   Sell it for money. ⌐

Not   Give you twenty roubles for it. ☉

Not   Alright then, twenty-five. ✳

Not   Swap it for something. ♐

Not   Trade it. ɑ

Not   Ten dollars to one chair on the open market. ♊

Not   Burn it for heat. ❋

Not   Smash it up. ⌘

Not   Blow it up. ⊠

Not   Yeah! ☢

Human   But imagine what else. 😩

Not   An upside-down chair. ?

Human   Yes, but what else? 😩

Not   A backwards chair? ◀

Human   Could it be a rocket ship? 😋

Not   No! ▪

Human   An elephant? 😕

Not   Don't be stupid. ◉

Human   Woah! 🙈

Human   What else? 🙄

Not   A chair on its side. φ

Human   😩

Not   It's a chair. φ

Human   😩

Not   It's a chair. φ

Human   😩

Nots (*all*)   A chair. ɸ

💪

💪

💪

💪

💪

💪

Human   This isn't going very well. 😔

Not   How do you know? ⚖️

Human   Just a hunch. 😐

Not   What's a hunch? ▭

Human   A feeling. 😶

Not   Everything's brilliant. //

Human   *Some* things are brilliant. 😶

Human   Some things are *not* brilliant. 😐

Not   Don't you hate it when Error 404. ①

Human   That's not what I mean. 😖

Not   Don't you hate it when User Not Found. ①

Human   What? 😳

😳😳😳

Human   Perfect or imperfect? 😶

Not   Perfect skin. ▱

Not   Perfect perfect. ◺

Human   Certain or uncertain? 😶

Not   Certain for sure. ◁

Human   Happy or famous? 😶

Not   Famous is happy. ▷

Human   Rich or loved? 😶

Not   Money is love. ☑

Not   Love is money. ◿

😣

Human   We have a problem here. ✋

⚫

👎

Human   Tell the humans here (*the audience*) what you feel.
🙂

Not   This account has been temporarily disabled. ⇐END

Human   Talk to everyone here. (*The audience.*) 😌

Not   Virus detected. ⇐END

Human   Go on. 😶

Not   Unable to install application. ⇐END

A stand-off.

*The **Not**s on the stage.*

*The **Human**s in the audience.*

Human   Hey. ✋

Human   Hey. ✋

Human   Why don't you come and join us? 🖐

Nots (*all*)   😶

Human   I've got a good idea. 💡

Human   Come over here and join us. 😶

Nots (*all*)   😶

Human Come on. 😶

Human Hold our hands. 🤝

Human You said you were our friends, remember. 🧑

Human Yeah. ☝️

Human I'm feeling a bit sad, I could do with a hug. 🧑

Human Me too. ☝️

Human A hug would be nice. 🧑

Human Yeah. ☝️

Human I'm confused about things. 🧑

Human Give us all a hug. 🧑

Not 😶

Human Can't hear you. 😩

Not 😶

Human Join us. 🌊

Not Something went wrong. ♨️

Human What went wrong? 😕

Not This image is no longer available. ❎⌘❎

Human What image? 😕

Not Bad file request. ❎⌘❎

Human Come and be with us. 😕

Not Authorisation required. 😬

Human You have it. 😫

Human We gave it to you. 😫

Human And a quid. 😩

Not An error has occurred. ❎⌘❎

Human   Tell us about it. 😑

Not   File not found. ❎⌘❎

Human   This is rubbish. 😶

Not   Out of memory. ❎⌘❎

Human   What are you talking about? 😤

Not   Crash. ❌

Not   Crash. ❌

Nots (*all*)   CRASH. ❌

*The **Not**s crash. This shouldn't be like robots breaking down! Just the actors playing the **Not**s stop!*

👆 😵

Human   Audience. 👆

Human   Hey, audience. 👋

Human   Audience. 👆

Human   Show us a robot. 🤖

Human   Yes. 👍

Human   Okay, audience. 👆

Human   Audience. ✊

Human   Select all squares that contain robot. 🤖

Human   Select all images with robot. 👉

Human   Hey, audience. 📱

Human   Audience. 🌀

Human   Shut this down. 😎

Human   Hey, audience. 👐

Human   Switch this off. 😎

Human   Audience. 🙌

Human   Log off. 😎

⬅️⬅️⬅️
END END END

🌝🌚🌝

Human   Come for a walk with us. 🐾

Human   Let's go feed the ducks. 🦆

Human   Or something. 🌝

Human   Let's fill our lungs with fresh air. 🌬️

Human   Come on, audience. 🌝

Human   Yes! Come on! 😃

Human   Let's look for shapes in the clouds. ☁️

Human   Let's have some cake. 🍰

Human   Or an apple. 🍎

Human   I don't like apples. 🌝

Human   Cake then. 🌝

Human   Cake! 🍰

Human   Let's lie down on the grass. 🌱

Human   Let's wrap up warm. 🧣

Human   Let's put some sun cream on. 🌞

Human   Let's get it wrong. 🌝

Human   Let's work it out together. 🌝

Human   Let's be humans. 😇

Human   Come with us. 🍰

Human   Let's go. 🌝

💜💜💜

*The **Human**s and the audience leave together.*

The **Not***s are left by themselves.*

End.

Ms Campbell's Class
Fifth Period
by Leyla Josephine

Characters

The characters are designed so anyone can play them, you're more than welcome to make adjustments and change pronouns.

Mack *is the class clown, the troublemaker. They love showing off and making people laugh, even if it means ruffling a few feathers.*

Clover *likes everything done a certain way. Their way. They are always keen to please – well, they like to please those who matter; everyone else can get lost.*

Bell *likes to stay out of things. Keep their head down. They don't say much. In fact, they've not said anything for years.*

Ms Campbell *loves poetry and the sound of her own voice. You can choose someone to act as her or she could be a voice recording, or a lighting trick, or maybe she's a puppet that you create out of paper mache! Let your imagination run wild. You can also change her to a male character if that suits better.*

The Janny *works long hours in the school and can't be bothered with anything, except cats,* **The Janny** *loves cats.*

The **Chorus** *is made up of the rest of* **Ms Campbell**'*s class and should be made up of actors that aren't playing* **Bell**, **Mack** *or* **Clover**. *They'll be asked to invent their characters with the included character exercises. They'll also be asked to come up with their own lines – these sections are clearly marked. You can decide whether the written dialogue for the* **Chorus** *is distributed or said in unison or a mixture of both, or if you have another idea go for that! The text is just a starting point.*

*Sometimes if it's just one voice saying the line, rather than in unison, it might be appropriate to change the line so it suits that choice, e.g. 'we heard' might make more sense as 'I heard'.

Set

Everyone in the cast should have a chair. Think of the chairs as your scaffolding to create images, moments of movement and different shapes. They could also be a tool to show who has more power in the room at what time. There's opportunity to create some fun dynamics with them.

Empty chairs face the audience.

There is a sound of a bell ringing.

One by one, or in small groups, students buzz into the classroom and take a seat. There is a whir of activity and it should feel like lots of things are happening at the same time. The actors should think about what their character would be doing while they wait for the teacher to arrive.

Chorus

The story starts the same as each fifth period does.

The end of lunch hits with a kick, a buzz.
We're hyper from the sugar, manic from the fizz.
We're all screaming, running, laughing, slamming each
    other into walls.
Paper airplanes fly down the corridor, someone's blocked
    the loo with paper towels.

Monster Munch is stuck in-between braces, illegal chewing
    gum is being chewed.
The dinner ladies scrape plates, binning mushed-up
    left-over food.
There's a group recording a TikTok dance, one guy is
    doing the splits.
Someone's getting a uniform mark, groaning 'Again? Sir,
    you can't be serious?!'

We're on a high, it doesn't get much better than this.
Laughing until our sides hurt, taking the mick.
There's nothing better: getting to spend every day with
    your mates.
If it was lunch all day, we'd never leave this place.

But the fun doesn't last forever and next period is the
    worst.
Book us on the next rocket ship out of this universe.
It's only for dummies, the kids who come last.
It's time for Ms Campbell's Fifth Period English Class.

It's not that we're not smart, it's not that we're not able.
It's just so boring, we're worried it could be fatal.
We just can't be bothered, we just can't be assed.
Welcome to hell: Ms Campbell's Fifth Period English Class.

She's a rubbish teacher.
She doesn't explain anything right.
She's always pissed about something.
Always talking to herself or looking for a fight.
She purposely uses big words that we don't understand.
If you get stuck with her, you don't stand a chance.

We heard she murdered her ex and then made him into
    stew.
We heard she was caught smoking in the staff loos.
We heard she got fired from her last teaching post.
One stern look from her can turn bread into toast.

We heard she smacked a pupil.
We heard she's just got divorced.
We heard she's on Tinder. *Bleugh.*
She's never given a decent report.

We heard she force fed a pupil wine gums until they
    were sick.
We heard she once shouted so hard she grogged in
    someone's face.
We heard she's got devil horns under her hair.
She's something straight from a Primary 1's nightmare.

Mack *enters the room with a swagger.*

Chorus
    Here comes Mack.
    Maybe they'll cause trouble today and we can just sit back.

Mack   Alright troops, what's happening?!

Chorus
    Mack, do you think you'll do something bad today?
    Come on, do us a solid.
    We can't be arsed, we can't be bothered.

It's probably Charles Dickens or god forbid, Hamlet again.
Who cares about these ancient-old, dead-boring men?!

Mack   What more do you want from me? I'm knackered,
it's been a long day of trouble already. I've been late to all my
classes, I glued Mr Norris's lunch to his desk, I let the P5
hamster, Graham, loose at break *and* I've just put wee Paddy
the first year in the bin for the third time this week.

Chorus
Oi come on, just a wee thing, enough to send her on
   a rant.
Go on, go on, go on, do it for us, Mack.

Mack   Well, I suppose I could think of something.

Chorus   Yes, Mack! You're the best.

Mack   Well, she certainly wasn't impressed when I said she
had a face like a tuna baguette.

Chorus
Some of your finest work yet.
If that isn't poetry, we don't know what is.   .
We didn't even lift a pencil that period, the telling off went
   on for so long.
Go on, Mack, we're all behind you, do something wrong.

Mack   Well, if it's what my fans want . . .

Clover *enters pushing people out the way to get to their seat.*

Clover   Emmmm hello?! If you were walking any slower,
you'd be going backwards – MOVE.

Chorus
And here's Clover, a snob, always sticking to the rules.
Determined to get out of this town, they think they're too
   good for this school.
Their prefect badge twinkling in the florescent light.
Never happy unless they are proved right.

Clover   Did you do the homework last night? What did you get?

Chorus
We heard they've got a skyrocket IQ.
We heard they don't do anything but study after school.
We heard they're going to Oxford or Cambridge.
Ha, no chance, not if they keep failing English.   ·

Clover   I just didn't know what the questions wanted from me! It made no sense!

Chorus   Always blaming the teacher, or the school, or the *'choice of text'*.

Mack   Clover, are you sure you're not just bad at English?!

Clover (*rolls their eyes but doesn't rise*)   I swear if this affects my UCAS, I'll march right up to the head's office and tell all about what I really think of this stupid, stupid subject. Why would Hamlet wait so long to kill Claudius?! Surely he would have saved us all some time if he'd just got on with it and killed the guy. And Ms Campbell hasn't explained any of it. I don't understand how she got this job.

Chorus   We can't argue with that. She is total crap.

Bell *enters and makes their way to their seat.*

Mack   Alrrright Bell, what's happening?

Bell, *wearing noise cancelling headphones, ignores* **Mack** *and sits down.*

Chorus
Why does Mack even bother with Bell?
They always keep themselves to themselves.
Their headphones glued on.
Apparently they're easily 'overwhelmed'.
They never want to talk. They never say hi.
None of the adults have ever explained,
They've never told us why.

Clover   You shouldn't make fun of people, Mack.

Mack   I'm not! I'm just talking to my pal.

Chorus
We heard Bell's not talked for five years now.
We heard it's been their whole life.

Mack   Bell spoke in Primary.

Chorus
Nah, Mack don't tell lies.
We heard it was a violent incident.
We heard it was a car accident.
We heard it was all for attention.
We heard it was an allergic reaction.

Mack   Yeah, to Clover's bad chat.

Chorus   OOOOOOOHHHHHH Clover, are you gonna take that?!

Clover   Ha ha, good one. You been googling bad comebacks?

Mack   Shut it, Clover, ya lump of butter. You don't know anything.

Clover   I can see the joke you were trying to make. But Clover – the brand of spreadable vegetable fat – is *technically*, margarine. And that is a perfect example of how I know more than you and that micro-shrew brain of yours.

Mack   Are you calling me a shoe?

Mack *heads towards* **Clover** *but some class members hold them back.*

Clover   My point exactly.

Chorus
Quick everyone, sit down, Ms Campbell is on her way.
We wonder what kind of mood she'll be in today.

The class all sit on their chairs . . . except for **Mack**. **Ms Campbell** *enters the class room.*

Ms Campbell   Mack, why are you wandering the classroom, are you lost? Do you need a map? I take it you still haven't managed to get that brain transplant?

Mack *sits in their chair.* **Clover** *sits up, straightens their tie and clears their throat.*

Clover   Happy Monday, Ms Campbell, did you have a nice weekend?

Mack *mimics* **Clover** *behind their back.* **Ms Campbell** *looks at* **Clover** *suspiciously.*

Ms Campbell   I don't do weekends. Weekends are for the weak. My brain does not take breaks.

Clover   And that is why it is in such great shape.

The class groan at **Clover***'s see-through charm.*

Ms Campbell   Okay, now Clover has got their vestibule olfactory out of my gluteus maximus, I am pleased to announce that today is the day you take the test to decide what English set you will be in next year.

The class groan. **Clover***'s hand shoots up.*

Chorus
  Miss! Miss! Miss!
  You can't be serious?!
  This is a surprise, we've had no time to prepare.
  You mean to tell us, if we fail this test we have you for
    another year?
  You never warned us. This isn't fair!

Ms Campbell   I don't know if you're aware, but it is not my responsibility to keep you up to date with every little resolution I make. You are not children anymore. You should be taking more responsibility for your studies and knowledge, rather than just preparing for exams. You should be reading and thinking for the exuberance of it. This is what is wrong with the youth of today – no drive, no morals, no role models, fixed to their mobile devices. I read there was more applicants for Love Island, than university last intake. Disgusting. No wonder you're all going bald so early, there's no heat in the head!

Chorus
Look at Clover, they're sweating in panic.
Being the best is all they care about.

Mack   It's tragic.

Ms Campbell   Now, if you can all locate your copy of Robert Burns' 'Tam O'Shanter' and put away your textbooks and mobile devices, which should not be out in the first place.

Clover *stretches their hand even further in desperation to be noticed.*

Chorus (*whispering*)
If Clover stretches their hand any further.
They're going to surely dislocate their shoulder.

Ms Campbell   In fact, you can put them in the box on my bureau, and you can get them at the end of the day, as there is no need for you to have them at all.

The class groan. **Clover** *is practically jumping now.* **Ms Campbell** *clears her throat and starts reciting 'Tam O'Shanter' with much gusto.*

Ms C
When chapman billies leave the street,
And drouthy neebors neebors meet,

The class are rolling their eyes, making faces. This is not the first time they've heard this poem.

Ms C
As market-days are wearing late,
And folk begin to tak the gate;

Clover *manically swings their arms.*

Mack   Miss, I think Clover has a questi–

Ms Campbell   Don't interrupt me while I am performing!
While we sit bousin, at the nappy,

And gettin fou and unco happy
We think na on the lang Scots miles,
The mosses, waters –

Clover *is making strange noises in desperation. She can't ignore them anymore.*

Ms Campbell   Oh . . . for Shakespeare's sake . . . what is it Clover?!

Clover   Miss, you can't do this, I haven't had time to study. The poem is 250 lines long and it's not even in English. If I . . . if I . . . if I fail this test, I'll have to sit the lower level exam next year and I won't have enough time to climb to the grade I need by my final year at school. Which means I'll have to do English AT COLLEGE. Which will put me back a year for my applications, and that never ever looks good according to this live webinar on TEDx I listened to and I won't get into any of my top three choices and I'll end up in like Birmingham, or Dundee and the only person my age will be some guy called Gregory who took a *gap yah* and won't stop talking about how *lit* some stupid Moon Party was and boasting about how his mum still can't get the neon paint out his elephant tank top, and how *epic* and *awesome* everything is or was . . . or worse, maybe they'll look at my application and think, what idiot can't get their English and it might mean I don't get to uni at all and I will be disowned and . . . and . . . and I will have to work in . . . (*In horror.*) hospitality . . .

Mack *is mimicking* **Clover** *behind their back.* **Ms C** *looks down her nose at* **Clover** *now they've finished rabbiting.*

Ms Campbell   Maybe some life experience might put things into perspective, Clover.

Clover   I beg you, give me another day and I promise I –

Ms Campbell *holds up her hand to stop them.*

Ms Campbell I'm sure you could get a job in a Subway sandwich shop, apparently they have really great managerial training and you can move right up the ranks.

Mack Plus they have pretty steezy hats. My sister worked in the one in the garage at the Lauriston Roundabout and loved it, she could make any sandwich at any time she wanted and any combination. She once had tuna and ham! *Together* . . . FOR FREE. Revolutionary. Not to mention open access to refills. Once, I went in for a Fanta and she made me drink it straight from the tap and it was dyno . . . even though I did feel a bit boak after and had bubbles up my nose for a week. You get decent wage too, a job not to be snuffed at.

Ms Campbell And who knows, one day, your boss might be a waste of breath like Mack.

Clover Miss, please, I don't want to mix my food in disgusting combinations I wan–

Ms Campbell *CLOVER*, stop whining. Now, I am going back to my recital, and it might do some of you good to actually *LISTEN. LISTEN.*

She taps her ears. **Mack** *imitates* **Ms Campbell** *and* **Bell** *smirks.*

Ms Campbell Do you have something to say Bell?

Ms Campbell *waits.* **Bell** *says nothing of course.*

Ms Campbell No, I didn't think so. Take those ridiculous headphones off.

Everyone takes a sharp inhale. There is silence. **Bell** *looks shocked.*

Chorus
We can't believe she just said that.
It's just Bell's thing, their safety blanket.
Everyone, even the other teachers, just kind of respects it.

Ms Campbell Are your ears also not working?

Everyone avoids eye contact – that was out of line.

Ms Campbell   You think you can laugh when you want behind my back? Smirk at me? Make fun of me? But refuse to participate properly? You think you're special but I'm onto you and I think this is all a way to –

Mack   Miss, I think you should just leave it.

Ms Campbell   What?

Mack   I said, I think you should just leave it.

Chorus
    Oh no, Mack. You're braver than us.
    She's not in the mood, don't throw yourself under the bus.
    We take back our previous request, we wouldn't start on
       her today.
    Bite your tongue, for once, just go with her flow – sit tight
       and obey.

Ms Campbell *approaches a shifty* **Mack**.

Ms Campbell   You think you run this school, don't you?

She waits for an answer but it doesn't come.

Ms Campbell   Don't you?

Mack   Emmm, I sup–

Ms Campbell   Well, school isn't real life. And when you leave here you'll soon find out how insignificant you truly are. You are nothing but a clown, Mack. Clowns often have an audience, I'll give you that. But clowns are never in a pair, never part of a group. Clowns are always alone, have you noticed that, Mack? Their only service is to be laughed at, not with. You like to show off in front of your peers and I know you're the same in every class. But I see you walking home alone. And I know your kind. I know you will leave here with no prospects, no real friends. You think you're different, special, but I've seen students like you a million times before. You have nothing but attitude to give and that is of no value to the system when you leave here. You will amount to nothing in the grand scheme of things. You will not matter to any –

Blackout.

There is a loud bang and shouting but nothing is clear. A woman screams. People are running around moving chairs.

The lights go on and everyone is in new positions, shocked, frozen. **Ms Campbell** *is nowhere to be seen.*

Chorus

What just happened? It was hard to tell.

It was hard to see with the lights off. It was hard to hear above the yells.

Something is missing. Something doesn't feel quite right.

Something has gone wrong. We've got chills up our spines.

We're confused. We don't know who did it.

Was it planned? Was it calculated?

It was all so rushed, so haphazard.

But Ms Campbell has been locked in the stationery cupboard.

Everyone turns and looks at **Mack**.

Mack   It wasn't me!

Clover   Of course it was you! It's always you! Oh lordy, lordy, lordy.

You're going to get into so much trouble for this. You're done, you're expelled, this is it my friend, your last straw!

Mack   How could it have been? Everyone was looking at me?

Clover   I'm not going down for this. Na uh. No siree. Nada. Njet. Nope. No. No. No. Nej. Nien. No. Nope I'm not getting involved. I'm going to tell another teacher right now.

Clover *heads towards the door but some other pupils block them.*

Chorus

It usually would be you, Mack.

It's the kind of thing you'd do.
If we were basing this on history.
Our money would be on you.

Mack   It wasn't me!

The rest of the class shake their heads.

Chorus
Mack, you've gone too far this time.
Mack, you've well and truly crossed the line.
Mack, there is no way we can back you on this.
Mack, you're by yourself in this shit.

Mack   I didn't do anything! Someone back me up.

Mack *looks at* **Bell**. **Bell** *looks at the floor, doesn't say anything.*
Mack *looks gutted.*

Mack   What about Bell, they were the one being made to
do something they didn't want to do.

Bell *holds up their hands and shakes their head. As if to say 'It
wasn't me'.*

Clover   You're always picking on someone, just give it a rest.

Chorus   Yeah, Mack.

Mack   What are you talking about, man, I was the one
standing up for Bell, while you all sat back.

Clover   Why would I get involved with something that
doesn't concern me?

Bell *points at* **Clover**. *The class gasp.*

Mack   You!

Clover   Pffft. Me? . . . Me? Don't be ridiculous. You think
I'd risk it all . . . my future, my potential, my ten year plan,
for what?

Mack   I was sitting right here, it must have been one of
you!

Mack *points at the rest of the class.*

Chorus
> Don't look at us, Mack.
> Sure, we didn't help her.
> But we didn't orchestrate the attack.

Mack   All I know is, it wasn't me.

The whole class look at each other suspiciously.

Chorus
> We don't know who it was.
> We'll admit the situation is blurred.
> It doesn't change the fact that Ms Campbell is locked
> in the cupboard.
> What do we do? What do we do? What do we do?

Mack   Well, the first thing we need to work out is: have we killed our teacher?

Clover   OH MY GOD WE'VE KILLED HER!

The class go into a frenzy. When they eventually calm themselves, they all tip-toe towards the door and listen.

Chorus
> Nothing. Silence. Maybe we have killed her.
> Maybe she bumped her head, maybe she took a seizure.
> How on earth are we going to explain this?
> Our parents are going to be so mad, they are going to
> be so pissed.

There is a small groan from the cupboard.

Clover   She's alive. Hallelujah. She's alive.

Chorus
> We're not sure if that's good or bad.
> We don't condone violence but it's hard to be 100 per
> cent glad.
> When she was dead at least we could say whatever we
> wanted.
> Now she's alive, she'll definitely hunt and kill us.

Mack (*speaking like a preacher*)   Settle down. Settle down, my fans, my people. Even though this wasn't me (*crosses their heart*) I am happy to take the role of 'Oh Important Leader'. And I think even though it might be hard to see right now, I think this is a good thing. Think of this as an opportunity. A prayer answered. A wish granted. We finally got what we all desired.

Chorus

We suppose that's true but it's hard to remember what we wanted . . .

Can you remind us what that was? Now that we have got it?

Mack   FREEEEDOOOOOM

DEVISING MOMENT

Everyone breaks out into celebration – maybe the class trash the place, maybe they rave, maybe they wrestle, maybe they pop alcohol-free champagne. Whatever you think the class would do in this moment of joy, of freedom. Do it. Well, everyone except Clover who is not into the joy aspect of things. It should feel loud, vibrant, funny. It should all stop suddenly when there are footsteps in the corridor.

Chorus

Wait, can you hear that?
Footsteps in the corridor.
Quick, someone is coming.
ACT NATURAL.

The whole class freeze in forced natural positions. Think the mannequin challenge from 2016 (if you're old enough to remember it). The footsteps pass, everyone relaxes and bursts into hysterical laughter.

Mack   See, I told you, I think this is a good thing.

Clover (*under breath*)   You would.

Mack   What did you say?!

Clover   I said, *you would!*

Mack   What's that supposed to mean?

Clover   It means you're an IDIOT! It means Ms Campbell was right. You only live in the moment and never think about consequences. We are in serious trouble. Do you not understand that? We have kidnapped and maybe seriously hurt someone, someone who doesn't even like being asked a question, never mind bundled into a cupboard and locked up by snotty, spotty, sweaty teenagers!

A few pupils smell their armpits.

And you're all dancing around like it's a game! This isn't one of Mack's wind ups, this is an actual crime.

Mack (*quietly*)   Don't call me an idiot.

Clover   You're . . .

Mack   Don't

Clover   An . . .

Mack   I'm warning you

Clover   Idi–

Mack *heads towards* **Clover***, the class intervene again*

Chorus
    Calm down, calm down, let's not fight.
    We need to work out what to do.
    We need our heads screwed on tight.
    We need to stick together or we'll be suspended.
    We need to get our story straight, do our best to avoid
        punishment.

Mack   If you're so smart, Clover, what should we do?

Clover   I think we should let her out and whoever did this should own up to it and deal with the consequences.

Mack   And what if no one owns up?

Chorus
>We need a reasonable reason to explain how she ended
>   up in there.
>An excuse we can agree on, blame we can share.
>It looks bad if we've just done it out of malice.
>What if we say we had no other option; it was self-defence?

Mack   No, they'd never buy that . . . one teacher against a whole class?

Clover (*under their breath*)   And a reprobate one at that.

Chorus   What if we said she was torturing us with her boringness?

Mack   Which is not untrue.

Chorus
>Still, locking her away is not a reasonable conclusion to
>   come to.
>What if we said she was a danger to herself?

Mack   That she had been manically smacking her head off the bookshelf?

Clover   She would just tell the adults that was nonsense.

She'd say that she was perfectly sane and the accusation was ridiculous.

Chorus   What if we said it was a strike or a protest situation?

Mack   That's genius!

Chorus   Kids are always getting praise these days, for standing up for what they believe in.

Mack   We could say we're not happy with what we have learned.

Chorus   Use this to be the change we want to see in the world.

Clover (*rolling their eyes*)   That's a new one. Violent abduction, sponsored by Gandhi.

Mack   The guy from Lord of the Rings? What's he got to do with Ms Campbell in a cupboard?

Clover   Good grief.

Mack   I could never get into anything with ogres, puts me right off my tea.

Chorus
We could use this opportunity to make a point.
We've been fed up for ages about how things are run in
    this joint.

The computers are all broken.
The staff are in bad moods.
The carpets are full of dust.
The cafeteria might as well be selling dog food.

The florescent lights flicker.
The ranks are rigged.
Pupils like us are stuffed to the bottom.
Sacrifices on a sinking ship.

If we had control there's a lot of things we'd change.
Things we'd get rid of, things we'd rearrange.
We could say the kidnapping was all planned!
Go on a live stream and list our demands

DEVISING MOMENT

Write a list of your own dreams for the education system and use them as a starting point to write a new piece of text for the class.

Ask yourself: what changes in the education system would I like to see? If you were in charge, what kind of school would you like to build – maybe pupils are organised into interests or learning styles rather than ages, maybe you'd like to have different subjects available (what?), maybe you'd like slides instead of stairs, or a Starbucks in the cafeteria, maybe you think all classes to be taught online or maybe you'd like to get paid to go to school? Let your mind run riot.

Choose a selection of funny and serious ones. The characters should list them off while building their dream school with chairs. Decide who should say what depending on the character you've created. If you can make them rhyme great, but if not, don't worry. During this, towards the end, the pupils should start yawning, stretching and slumping. The class are nodding off on their chairs. Someone falls off their seat and naps under their desk.

Clover   What's happening? Why are you all so tired all of a sudden?

Chorus

    Oh no, here it comes the afternoon slump.

    The hangover from the sugar, the comedown from the buzz.

    We always thought it was Ms Campbell's chat that made us nod off.

    We should have predicted this but . . . (*Yawn.*)

Mack (*yawning*)   I shouldn't have had . . . that chips and cheese and curry sauce after all . . . but it was so (*fighting to stay awake*) it was sooo . . . goo (*Yawn.*) . . . no . . . regrets . . .

Mack *falls asleep too.*

Clover   This is why you need to have a packed lunch with all major food groups covered and limit sugar or your stomach uses all your energy to digest and leaves you no energy to . . . to . . . (*realising they've been left alone*) oh no . . .

oh no . . . guys? Wake up, wake up. Please, don't leave me alone with Ms Campbell in a cupboard.

Bell *is the only other person still awake.*

Clover   Packed lunch?

Bell *nods.* **Clover** *goes around trying to wake everyone up.*

Clover (*to* **Bell**)   Help me?

Bell *shrugs and folds their arms.* **Clover** *hears footsteps again and looks out in the corridor.*

Clover (*whispering furiously*)   Everyone wake up. Wake up! Someone's coming. Oh no, it's The Janny. If they realise it's going to be the end of me.

Clover *runs to the door before they come in.*

Janny   What's going on here?

Clover *looks over their shoulder at the class sleeping.*

Clover   Emm, emmm, it's emmm, I, well, the thing is, we were just . . .

Stuttering and unable to speak, **Clover** *is extremely anxious, sweating. They hate lying, especially to an adult.*

Janny   You have five seconds to tell me exactly what's going on here.

Clover *looks like they're about to spurt everything out.*

Clover   Well, I can explain –

Bell *appears at* **Clover**'s *side and gives them a piece of paper.* **Clover** *reads it.*

Clover   Yes. Yes . . . of course, thank you, Bell. I momentarily forgot the name of the exercise that we are doing . . . Sir, it's our weekly session on . . . (*squints at papers*) trans . . . transidential, (*more confident*) transcendental meditation.

Janny   Wit?

Clover   Transcendental meditation. Stress techniques for exams. Ms Campbell is a big advocate to lower study-related stress in teenagers, didn't you know?

Janny   Is she now?

Clover   Yes.

Janny   And where is Ms Campbell?

Clover   She's transcended . . .

Bell *digs their elbow into* **Clover**'s *stomach.*

Clover   Ow. Sorry, no, I mean . . . she's gone to give Mr Smart, some . . . emm some . . . some smart board batteries.

The Janny *looks at them suspiciously, raising their eyebrows.*

Janny   She's gone to give some smart board batteries to Mr Smart?

Clover *and* **Bell** *nod vigorously.*

Janny   Hmmm. Okay, well tell her I called, I'll come back at the end of the day about the bulb she needs.

The Janny *sets off,* **Bell** *and* **Clover** *silently celebrate.* **The Janny** *turns around.*

Janny   One more thing . . .

Bell *and* **Clover** *stop celebrating.* **The Janny** *walks slowly towards the pair.*

Janny (*whispering*)   Does it work? This translucent medication thing? . . . Things have been awful fraught at home since my cat Dolly got run over and I'm finding myself a little more . . . a little more . . . I can admit it these days . . . *weepy* . . . than usual.

Clover *and* **Bell** *look at each other, nod their heads and give a sympathetic smile.*

Janny   Hm, must try it sometime. Okay, cheerio.

The Janny *walks away.*

Clover   Phew. Thanks, Bell. How did you come up with that one?

Bell *chuckles and shrugs. The rest of the class start to yawn and wake up.*

Chorus
>What just happened? Did Clover just lie to a staff
>   member?
>Did Bell actually get involved?
>Things have sure flipped around here,
>Since Ms Campbell's been in that cupboard.

The class look impressed.

Mack (*putting their arm around* **Clover**)   Nice one, mate!

Clover *looks pleased for a second and then checks themselves.*

Clover (*shrugging them off*)   I'm not your mate.

Mack   Well, you're certainly not the same goody-two-shoes that walked into the room are you, Marge?

Clover   Marge?

Mack   Yeah, Marge . . . MAARGE.

Mack *looks to the rest of the class for encouragement.*

Clover   What?

Mack   Marg-ah-rine . . .

Mack *cackles, but the rest of the class look blank.* **Mack** *tries to explain the joke through giggles.*

Mack   You know, like butter, margarine, Marge, Clover, the brand, you get it?!

Mack *notices that the rest of the class aren't reacting; they get it, but they've had enough.*

Mack   Come on, that's a good one! What's up with you all?

Still nothing. **Mack** *looks bashful and stops laughing.*

Pause.

Clover   You need to own up to this.

Mack   Me?

Chorus
Yes, Mack, you. We've not changed our position.
It's time you own up and take the blame for this situation.

Mack   No way, I didn't do anything. Why should I?

Clover   Because it doesn't make a difference to your life.

Mack   You actually think that?

Clover   Yes, I do.

Mack *looks at the rest of the class.*

Mack   You all think that?

The class say nothing. Their silence speaks volumes. **Mack** *thinks for a minute, they look upset but then a smug smile creeps on their face.*

Mack   I've got an idea . . . why don't we make this interesting . . . a bet . . .

Clover   No way.

Chorus
What's Mack got up their sleeve?
They've got that look in their eye.
No way are they going to let Clover say those things.
No way will they let those comments fly.

Mack   We split into two teams – I'm a team leader, and Clover is a team leader.

We play some games . . . and whoever loses overall takes the blame.

Clover   No way.

Chorus

Oh, this does sound interesting.

Since Clover thinks Mack is worthless and will amount to
nothing.

They should have no problem taking on some healthy
competition . . .

Clover   No. Nada. Not happening.

Chorus

Are you scared, Clover? Not up to the challenge?

Thought this would be your thing with all that brain
talent.

Thought you considered yourself the smartest of us all

But now it seems you're frightened with your back against
the wall.

Clover *looks at everyone, measuring up their likeliness of winning.*

Clover   Fine, but I get to pick first.

DEVISING MOMENT

Design your own classroom olympics. Come up with
different games the class could play to decide who takes
the blame between Clover and Mack. Think about
challenges that use the brain and challenges that use
the body. Then choose which ones should go into the
play. Bell can be referee and everyone else can choose
where they think their character's loyalties would lie.

Clover *and* **Mack** *pick their teams and shake hands.*

*The class are having so much fun and end up falling around
laughing. They forget why they're playing these competitions. There
is no clear winner. Even* **Mack** *and* **Clover** *look like they are*

enjoying each other's company. Suddenly there is a loud bang from inside the cupboard.

Chorus
> Oh no, Ms Campbell has just woken up.
> Sounds like she's raging and had enough.
> There's only ten minutes left until the period is over.
> We got distracted, who should we blame, Mack? or Clover?
> We need to get this sorted. Pronto. Quick. Hurry.
> Mack, can you just say it was you and that you're sorry?

Clover   Oh no, oh god. This is a nightmare.

Mack   Can you please just calm it? Let me think.

Clover   How can I calm it? I'm not like you. I'm not like any of you. I have prospects, aspirations. A chance to get out of here. My family they're relying on me. I want to actually do something with my life.

Mack   What makes you think we don't?

Clover   I don't believe what you were saying earlier about the school system being rigged. You all give up so easily and see yourself as victims before you've even given it a go. You don't try.

Mack   Yeah we do.

Clover   You don't care. I care. I don't deserve this. I shouldn't even be in a bottom set at all. You don't even pick up a pencil in most classes, Mack.

Mack   It's complicated.

Clover   How is it complicated?

Mack   You wouldn't understand, mate.

Clover   Try me.

Mack *says nothing.* **Bell** *is furiously writing something.*

Chorus
> It looks like Bell has something to say.
> They're scribbling on that piece of paper furiously.

DEVISING MOMENT

Find a way of saying or showing what Bell has written without them having to speak. Maybe you project the words, or another classmate reads it out for them, or maybe you have a better idea!?

Bell   School was created in the industrial revolution when factory and land owners wanted to keep their employees' kids busy so they could work longer. Then they realised they could use schools to create future employees, well-designed employees, ones that they could make the most out of. Our system hasn't updated in centuries. School teaches you how to obey orders, stay in line, respect authority, don't ask too many questions, like a perfect employee . . .

Clover   Hold on a minute –

Bell *holds up their hand and continues writing.* **Clover** *shuts up.*

Bell   Most school subjects teach you that there is one right answer to every problem which is the opposite of IRL.

Clover   IRL?

Mack   In real life.

Bell   . . . There are endless right answers and routes to get to that answer. The best inventors, makers, most successful business people make money by thinking out of the box, collaborating, taking risks but the public school system doesn't encourage that at all. They teach us how to sit exams. That there is only one right answer and you can't ask someone else, you can't google or research, you have to memorise it. Pupils leave school scared to death of making mistakes, paralysed. The government won't change the traditional structure, because they know it needs employees for society to function. It's different at the private schools, they learn how to be leaders, bosses. They learn it's okay to fail. We learn to be sheep, scared sheep. Our education system teaches you what to think, not how to think.

Bell *gestures a *mic drop*. There is a pause, everyone is gobsmacked taking this information in.*

Mack   Yeah, what Bell said! School sucks!

Clover *looks shellshocked.*

Clover   You wrote all of that down just there? It was all just in your brain ready to go . . . ?

Bell *nods and writes something down.*

Bell   I think a lot.

Clover   I'd never thought about any of that, the history and stuff . . . I just thought it was just the way it was because . . . well . . . I never actually considered it.

There's another bang from the cupboard and some shouting.

Chorus
We've got to get a move on.
Mack, you should take the blame.
We'll admit it's not ideal, it is a shame.

But why deny who you are,
You're always bending the rules.
The well-known-cheeky-chop, running riot in the school.

Go on, Mack, take this one for the team.
You can add it to your long list
Of fun and defiant schemes.

Go on Mack, do it for us.
Don't turn your back on who you are.
Let's be honest, you weren't going to make it to the end
of the year.

Mack *thinks for a moment.*

Mack (*sheepishly*)   Okay.

Chorus

Yes, Mack, our saviour, saves us again.

We won't forget about you when you're expelled and
    shipped off to Spain.

You're a legend, we all agree.

Mack, 'Our Important Leader' for eternity!

They all cheer. **Clover** *and* **Bell** *look unhappy about this.* **Mack**
*smiles a small smile but can't hide their disappointment that the class
are happy for them to take the blame.* **Clover** *looks at* **Mack** *and sees
how unhappy they are.*

Clover   Mack, this doesn't feel right.

Mack   Why do you care? It's what you wanted.

Bell *starts writing something down again.*

Clover   I know but –

Mack   As Ms Campbell said, and you said and as the whole
class said . . . my future looks grim anyway. What difference
will it make?

Bell *shoves a piece of paper to* **Clover***,* **Clover** *reads it.*

Bell   Mack is good at English.

Mack   Shut it, Bell.

Mack *grabs the paper from* **Clover***.* **Bell** *nods.*

Chorus

Nah, nooo way, it can't be true

Mack, is Bell taking the piss out of you?

Mack (*harsher*)   Shut it, Bell.

Bell *grabs* **Mack***'s workbook,* **Mack** *tries to block but fails and
hands it to* **Clover***.* **Clover** *scans it.*

Clover   What is this? What is all of this? Is this . . . is this . . .
is this POETRY?!

Mack *sighs and looks embarrassed.*

Mack   I like to think of it as more like 'rap' for the page.

Clover   What is this . . . you've got . . . you've got . . . you've got an A?!!!

Mack   Look, English is my thing! (*Quietly.*) Just don't tell anyone alright?

Clover   But you're in the bottom set?

Mack   Aye, for behaviour reasons only.

Clover   But I don't, I don't understand . . .

Mack   You're too logical, Clover, you've got to loosen up a bit, do a bit more *feeling*, y'know?

Mack *approaches and put their hand on* **Clover***'s chest.*

Mack   You got to write from the heart, explore what's happening in here?

Clover (*heavy breathing*)   Right now . . . in here? . . . I think I'm having a stroke.

Mack   Maybe I could help you sometime?

Clover   What?! Are you secretly medically trained as well?!

Mack   With English. Sure, Ms Campbell's strict, mean, with some old-fashioned, coo coo views and smells like Dragon Soop every Monday, but see those stories . . . those books she gives us, they're . . . well they're kinda class.

Clover   You like Robert Burns?

Mack   Oh god nah, even I hate him. But like, she kinda lets us think for ourselves. You just need to read the stories and explain how they made you feel

Clover   Frustrated.

Mack   If you can explain why you find it frustrating . . .

Clover   Well, because I don't know the right answer.

Mack   That's because there is no right answer . . .

Clover   But then how do I get it right?

Mack   There's no right answer, no, wrong answer, you just have to learn to back your answer up. Figure out why the writer wanted you to feel like that and how they did it. You've got to think for yourself.

Clover   I don't know how to do that . . .

Mack   I can show you, it's easy . . . we can look at some of your –

Banging on the door again, louder and lots of shouting with it.

Chorus

    Well isn't this cute and cuddly but time's up and we need
       to move.
    And we've still not found a culprit or an excuse.

Mack   I don't mind taking the blame, I really don't, but for real, just tell me who it was.

The class are silent. There is banging on the door again.

Mack   Come on.

The class all look at each other. **Bell** *slowly raises their hand. The class look shocked.*

Mack   Bell?

Bell *nods. They head for the lights and switch them on and off.*

Mack   You turned off the lights?

Bell *nods.*

Chorus

    Ah of course, old best friends sticking up for one another.
    They used to hang out all the time.
    Thick as thieves, shoulder-to-shoulder.
    But something happened when Bell went quiet.
    Mack started getting into trouble and Bell just sort of . . .
       drifted.

Mack   You did that for me? Why? You hate me?

Bell *shakes their head.*

Mack   You like me? Well, you've got a funny way of showing it, pal!

Bell *looks at the floor.* **Mack** *eases.*

Mack   Why do you never talk to me anymore? When we started secondary . . . you just . . . I thought I did something . . . I thought you didn't want to talk to me.

Bell *says nothing.*

Mack   What is it then? We used to have such a laugh. We've been pals since we were born and then . . . what happened?

Bell *says nothing.* **Mack** *thinks for a moment, then approaches* **Bell**.

Mack (*softly*)   You don't need to talk to me, Bell. You just need to hang out.

Bell *looks at* **Mack** *and smiles.*

Mack   You into that?

Bell *nods.* **Mack** *hugs them.*

Mack   It will be good to have you back. We can go to my dad's and drop eggs out the window like the good old –

More banging, this time some muffled yelling. The class jump and refocus on the issue at hand.

Chorus
　　If Mack was in their seat.
　　And Bell was at the lights.
　　Who did the pushing and locking?
　　Someone has something to hide.

The whole class spins and looks at **Clover**.

Clover   Okay, okay, ja, si. Oui, tak. yes. Yeah. OKAY. Yes. It was me. I admit it, it was me. I panicked. I didn't want to do the test and I just . . . I just . . . my feet were moving . . . my hands were grabbing . . . and before I knew it, bang. I'd ruined my whole life . . .

Mack   HA! I told you! I told you!

Clover   This is the end for me.

Mack   I didn't think you had it in you!

Clover   I'm sorry, Mack, I shouldn't have tried to get you to own up.

Mack   No, probably not.

Clover *sits with their head in their hands.* **Mack** *approaches and puts a hand on* **Clover***'s shoulder.*

Mack   Look, I'll take the blame.

Clover   No, that's not right. I will own up to what I did – they'll go easy on me anyway.

Mack   Well, I can say I helped if you like.

Bell *nods in agreement – they'll take the blame too.* **Clover** *looks at them both.*

Clover   You'd both do that for me?

Mack   Well, aye, well, naw, it's also because I'm a bit embarrassed. I've got a reputation to protect. This will go down in high school history and I won't even get a mention. It would be social suicide, can't have you and Bell taking all the cred.

Chorus
Why don't we all take our share.
We all had a part to play. It's only fair.
They can't expel the whole class.
No way would the school get away with that.

Mack   Are you all sure?

Chorus
Yes, we've got your back.
Things wouldn't be the same around here without you,
   Mack.

The banging and shouting starts up again.

Mack   It's nearly next period. It's now or never.

Bell *and* **Mack** *head towards the door.*

Mack   Ready?

Clover   Wait.

The class look at **Clover***.*

Mack   Don't tell me you've chickened out already?

Clover   Do you think we've got time to maybe . . . look at the answer for the test?

Mack   Well, well, well. We thought you'd decided you were going to do a bit of thinking for yourself, Clover?

Clover   Is that not exactly what I'm doing?

Mack   Yes! I suppose it is.

Clover   I learnt from the best.

Clover *nods at* **Mack***.*

DEVISING MOMENT

The class go into Ms Campbell's bag, through her emails and desk. What do they find? Family pictures? A diary? Private emails? Decide on four objects that reveal the kind of life she leads and why this makes her what she's like. Write dialogue for the class to explain what has been found. Ask yourself, why do people get angry and frustrated? Why can some people be cruel and unkind? Why might Ms Campbell find herself speaking to young people in the way she does? If it rhymes, great, but no worries if it doesn't.

Mack   Let's look.

Chorus

I guess we didn't know Ms Campbell at all.
It's hard to imagine teachers' lives outside these four walls.
Maybe we've judged her too harshly in the past.
Though it's hard to believe, maybe she was doing her best.

What's going to happen when this door opens?
Will things go back to normal or are they permanently
    broken?
Will Clover and Mack and Bell be friends?
Will we ever pass our English tests?

Time will tell, it always does.
The earth will spin just because.
Every morning billions of children will go to school.
And we'll sit and listen, just because we're told to.

And events like these, even though they seem to be a big
    deal.
Will soon fade to old memories and won't feel real.
We're on the cusp of something we can almost taste.
Grown-upness, adulthood, soon we'll be of age.

But for now we have to face the consequences for our
    actions.
And we know we're in for a bollocking for what happened.
We wonder if Ms Campbell will ever get over what we did
    to her.
We wonder if we'll see her back tomorrow at her desk, in
her chair.

We wonder if she'll find it funny – maybe, not – especially
    if she suffered.
We wonder if she'll ever forgive us for locking her in that
    cupboard

Mack   Ready?

Everyone nods and braces for impact.

Clover, **Bell** *and* **Mack** *all have their hand on the door handle.
They look nervous.*

Chorus   3, 2, 1.

They open the door. The lights go out. A bell rings.

End.

CHARACTER DEVELOPMENT

The chorus should create their own character on the following two pages. The core cast can also do this with their characters but they will have to base their work on the info that's already in the script.

Outline Task

A) On the outside of this drawing write what is externally seen about your character, e.g. body language, clothes, attitude. Ask yourself: how are they perceived by the outside world?

B) On the inside of this drawing write what is happening internally to your character, e.g. their thoughts, their home life, their fears, their hopes. Ask yourself: how do they feel and why?

Questionnaire Task

A)   What is your character's name?

B)   What is your character's age?

C)   What is your character's favourite food?

D)   What kind of music does your character like?

E)   What is your character's favourite place in the world?

F)   What is your character's favourite and least favourite subject at school?

G)   What is your character's home life like?

H)   Who are your character's friends?

I)   What are three positive personality traits of your character?

J)   What are three negative personality traits of your character?

K)   What is your character's biggest fear?

L)   What is a belief your character has about themselves which is not true?

M) How does your character feel about being in the bottom set of English?

N)   What are your character's hopes for the future?

O)   How does your character change from the start of the play to the end of the play?

The Day the Stampers United
by Sara Shaarawi

Notes on the text

Italics denotes movement which could be both physical and vocal.

[words spoken between brackets are through a speaker or some other machinery]

Indented denotes dialogue or external voices.

All other words are spoken as internal voices or narration and can be divided among the group as the company pleases.

'Words in between quotations are thoughts heard by the audience but not heard within the world of the play.'

(The WAREHOUSE RULES are to be re-written by the company. Every group gets to choose what an oppressive (for-profit) space has as its rules, and how those are changed/ rewritten for a free (for-community) space. I've written my own as an example but you can change it collectively.)

Workers assemble (it can be a straight line or not).

The space is dull and grey and damp.

In a place not far from here, is a big, vast, crowded warehouse.

In this warehouse there is shifty scaffolding built all the way up to the high ceilings.

In this warehouse there is heavy-duty machinery that is faulty sometimes and causes accidents.

In this warehouse there are rules.

We notice the big sign that says:

WAREHOUSE RULES

1. *Don't Speak While You Work*

2. *Don't Eat While You Work*

3. *Don't Smile While You Work*

4. *Only Wear Grey and Black*

5. *No Breaks Allowed (not even to pee)*

6. *Never Be Late*

7. *Stay Hydrated!*

Also in this warehouse, there are people working.

Preparing packages to go out for delivery.

Packages containing birthday presents, impulsive purchases and home essentials.

Packages containing alternative medicine, new outfits and self-care bath bombs.

Packages containing anniversary gifts, work shoes and books about anti-capitalism.

And the workers preparing these packages are split into three groups.

There are Stickers, who stick.

Stick, stick, stick.

There are Stackers, who stack.

Stack, stack, stack.

And there are Stampers, who stamp.

Stamp, stamp, stamp.

All day, every day.

Stick, stack, stamp.

Stick, stack, stamp.

It's in this specific warehouse where it happened first.

Some say that on the day the stampers united, it was hot.

Very hot.

Too hot.

And everyone's shirts got soaked through.

Some say that the day the stampers united, it was raining.

The roof leaked.

The floor flooded.

And everyone's socks got really wet.

What we do know for sure, is that the day the stampers united started the same as any other day.

Everyone arrived on time. Signed in. And began to work.

Stick, stack, stamp.

It didn't matter that Louise hadn't slept because she was up all night studying for exams.

It didn't matter that Gabriel's arm still hurt from an injury he got from football last week.

It didn't matter that Sarah was anxious about her mother being in the hospital.

They strapped on their trackers and got to work.

Stick, stack, stamp.

The workers were told they had to maintain the same rhythm.

Stick, stack, stamp.

They were told this was the system and if the rhythm was thrown off, the warehouse would collapse.

Stick, stack, stamp.

Everyone would lose their jobs.

Stick, stack, stamp.

And the billionaire who owned the place would be very, very unhappy.

Stick, stack, stamp.

So that's why they needed the trackers on the wrists.

Trackers that tracked everything.

How many packages they stuck, stacked and stamped.

Stick, stack, stamp.

It tracked where they moved and how fast they moved.

Track, track, track.

It tracked the length and topic of their conversations.

Track, track, track.

It tracked what they ate for lunch.

And how long it took for them to eat it.

Track, track, track.

Trackers that made sure they kept their pace and rhythm.

But they didn't track absolutely everything.

They didn't track Ellie's heart palpitations from all the energy drinks she drank to stay alert.

Or the tears Alan held back as he tried to get over a painful break up.

Or the number of deep breaths taken by Layla as she tried to calm her fears about dying.

Stick, stack, stamp.

Track, track, track.

Stick, stack, stamp.

Track, track, track.

Layla has been getting nightmares.

She's been losing sleep.

She dreams of mountains crumbling and cities sinking into the sea.

She dreams of dry, dry deserts and the scorching sun, no shade in sight.

At home Layla does what she can.

She recycles and cycles.

She's vegan.

She doesn't travel by plane or buy anything new.

She doesn't use plastic.

Her flatmate finds her unbearable.

Her family tease her and call her extreme.

But Layla really cares about this world, and she's terrified it will die.

It all seems so pointless though.

That's what's so scary.

Layla tries to concentrate.

> *Stamp,   stamp,   stamp.*

But it's hard.

Her socks are soaked through.

The water is still rising.

The heat making her dizzy.

> *Stamp,   stamp,   stamp.*

She is slowing down.

> *Track,   track,   track.*

It's a bit difficult to breathe.

The self-care robot, Mr B Happy, is dispatched.

It whizzes over to Layla.

Whizzzzz

Whizzz

Whiz

– Stamper 135, you are slowing down.

Layla hates Mr B Happy with a passion.

– Stamper 135, your performance is 12 per cent less than your monthly average.

'Layla, my name is Layla actually'

Is what Layla wants to say.

But she chooses not to.

She needs this work.

People here get fired for less.

- On a scale from 1 to 10 how calm are you? Ten being extremely calm, 1 being extremely not calm.

- Nine

That's all she says.

- Oh I'm sorry you feel that way. Have you tried to take a few breaths?
  Let's try in for 5, out for 7. Ready? Breathe in . . . 5 4 3 2 and 1. And out . . . 7 6 5 4 3 2 and 1.

In . . . 5 . . . 4 . . . 3 . . . 2 . . . 1. And out . . . 7 . . . 6 . . . 5 . . . 4 . . . 3 . . . 2 . . . 1.

- Great. Are we feeling better?
  Remember, we can't care for you if you can't care for yourself!

Stay hydrated.

Whiz

Whizzz

Whizzzzzz

Layla actually doesn't feel better at all.

                    Stamp,   stamp,   stamp.

The water rises. It reaches her ankles now.

'This isn't right.'

Someone should say something.

Layla takes deep breathes.

In for 5 . . .

Out for 7 . . .

The person to her right, Calum, joins her breathing.

Calum is worried about rent.

> *Stamp,   stamp,   stamp.*

The person to her left, Asma, joins her.

Asma is worried about her family's asylum claim.

> *Stamp,   stamp,   stamp.*

In for 5 . . .

Out for 7 . . .

The rhythm is off.

Mr B Happy isn't going to be happy.

– Your performance is 44 per cent less than your monthly average.

Water rising.

'This isn't right.'

Layla thinks about all the objects in the packages she's stamping.

These are gestures of love.

Track,

These are coping mechanisms.

Track,

These are rites of passage.

Track.

She can't blame people for wanting these packages.

– On a scale from 1 to 10 how calm are you?

But the water is rising.

> *Stamp,   stamp,   stampstamp.*

And Layla thinks about all the objects in the packages she's stamping.

These are also distractions.

Track,

Moments of weakness.

Track,

Results of manipulative advertising.

Track.

But she can't blame people for wanting some comfort.

For wanting some distraction.

For wanting some love.

The water is above her knees now.

'This isn't right.'

–   Stay hydrated.

The breaths are now short and sharp.

Layla looks up and smoke has filled the air.

People are collapsing into the water.

'This isn't right.'

She thinks it but can't say it.

        Stick,   stack,   stamp, stamp,stamp.

'We need to stop.'

Why can't she say it?

A voice comes through the speakers.

[Please remain calm.]

[We are dealing with extreme weather just now. You will not be able to go home safely, so we have adjusted the rota, you will now all be required to work the night shift.]

– What!

– No!

– That's not fair!

– This isn't safe!

[Rest assured that your safety is of utmost importance to us, you will each receive a swimming aid in case of the water rising further, and a facemask to protect you from the smoke. We cannot afford to lose business over this. People need their bath bombs and work shoes and books on resisting capitalism, otherwise how will they forget about this terrible weather. We cannot let mother nature win. Have a great day!]

– I need to go home.

– This is wrong!

– You can't do this!

– Do we at least get our phones back?

[Phones disrupt productivity. We can't let productivity drop. A productive community is a happy community.]

Water halfway up their thighs, the smell of ash in the air.

The workers get back to work.

Stick, stack, stamp.

Stick, stack, stamp.

Stick, stack, stamp.

All the workers except for one.

Layla.

'No.'

She thinks.

'No no no.'

The packages start to pile up.

Stick, stack

Stick, stack

Stick, stack

Whispers fill the warehouse.

– What's happening?

– What is she doing?

– Why isn't she stamping?

Layla stands there.

Unable to move.

She's trying.

She really is.

But she can't.

The fear.

It spreads.

From her toes to her ankles to her calves to the tips of her fingers.

From her wrists to her navel to her chest to the voice caught in her throat.

Stick, stack

The fear.

She can't speak.

Stick, stack

She can't move.

Stick, stack

She stands there frozen.

Watching the packages drop into the water.

Stick, stack, splash

That will cost her.

Stick, stack, splash

All that water damage.

They'll take it out of her wages.

And she won't be able to afford the heating again.

And then she'll freeze.

And maybe this time she'll actually freeze.

Maybe she'll become an icicle.

Or a snowman.

Or a snow queen.

Maybe freezing won't be that bad.

Stick, stack, splash

[Stamper 135, why have you stopped?]

Stick, stack, splash

[Stamper 135 please resume your work]

Stick, stack, splash

[Stamper 135, resume your work or we will have to remove you from the premises]

Stick, stack, splash

[STAMPER 135 ARE YOU LISTENING!]

'Layla.'

[THAT'S IT!]

'Layla. My name is Layla.'

[GET OUT]

That's all Layla can think of.

But she can't say it.

She tries again.

'Layla.'

'My name is Layla.'

Why can't she say it?

Go on.

[STAMPER 135 THIS IS UNACCEPTABLE!]

Say it.

–   LAYLA

Silence.

[What did you say?]

–   My name is not Stamper 135. My name is Layla.

More silence.

[It doesn't matter what your name is because you don't work here anymore]

–   What?

[Mr B Happy please remove Stamper 135]

–   No, you can't do that!

[We just did. There are others that need this job]

–   I need this job!

[Well, that's too bad]

Whizz, whiz, whizzz.

– NO! Don't touch me. I need this job, I need it. I'm just terrified. I'm terrified of the water and the smoke. Please! I won't be able to pay the bills. I will freeze! I'm scared. I'm scared of mountains crumbling and scorched dry deserts and cities sinking into the sea! I didn't do it on purpose. I just want to be safe! I just want us to be safe! I want the world to be safe!

The other stampers watch as Layla struggles to stay.

'This isn't fair.'

Thinks Mark.

'They can't just get rid of her like that.'

Thinks Alex.

'She's right.'

Thinks Helena.

'We do deserve to be safe.'

Thinks Ewan.

'This water is scary.'

'They can't treat her like this!'

'She just wants to be treated like a human being!'

'We all want to be treated like human beings.'

Think the stampers.

And then, just as Layla is being dragged out.

One by one . . .

[Stamper 289, Stamper 5, Stamper 67, Stamper 112, Stamper 19 what are you doing?]

They stop.

[Stamper 55, Stamper 78, Stamper 189, Stamper 3, Stamper 145, Stamper 99, Stamper 230, Stamper 14, Stamper 15,

Stamper 16, Stamper 34, Stamper 11, Stamper 220, Stamper 221]

All of them.

[Stamper 33, Stamper 24, Stamper 66, Stamper 10, Stamper 90, Stamper 89, Stamper 245, Stamper 125, Stamper 78, Stamper 77, Stamper 118, Stamper 187, has everyone lost their minds!]

They all just . . . stop.

– Let her go! She's one of us!

– We're not stamping anything until this water is dealt with.

– In fact, we're not stamping anything until we're safe.

– And well, no more working for hours and hours with no breaks.

– And no more Mr B Happy checks.

[Is that so? Well then, you're all fired! Get out of our warehouse.]

The stampers refuse to budge.

[Remove them! Get them out of here!]

The stampers are nervous and scared, but they do not move.

Then they begin to notice something strange . . .

Apart from the robotic screeches of the boss, it is silent.

There is no sticking.

There is no stacking.

– You hurt one of us, you hurt all of us.

[What is this? A rebellion?! Get back to work.]

– No.

– We're done working for you.

–   We're done working in these conditions.

–   We're done being treated like objects.

–   We're done being treated like we're worthless.

–   We built this warehouse.

–   So we're keeping it.

[You can't do that! You didn't pay for it did you?]

–   We can and we will.

–   We built it brick by brick, without us there wouldn't be a warehouse.

–   This place is ours now.

–   We don't like how you're running things around here.

–   Your system is rubbish.

[I'll call security! I'll call the police! I'll call the B Happy brigade!]

–   Go ahead.

And that's how the occupation of the warehouse begins.

The stampers unite.

The stickers unite.

The stackers unite.

And together they fight off attacks from security guards.

Stack, stick, stamp!

They fight off attacks from the police.

Stamp, stack, stick!

The B Happy brigade doesn't stand a chance.

Stick, stamp, stack!

They don't just fight the attacks.

They also split into three building groups.

They build drains.

Stamp, stick, stamp, stamp, stack.

Which drain out the water.

They build chimneys.

Stackstack, stackstack, stick, stackstampstamp. Stack. Stack. Stack.

To clear out the smoke.

They repair the damage done to the building.

Stick, stick   stick, stack   stick, stamp, stick

They work together.

In sync.

But each moving at their own rhythm.

And Layla can finally breathe again.

Mr B. Happy joins the occupation and now whizzes around offering people cold drinks and delicious snacks and chocolates.

Whizzzzz,   whiz, whiz, whiz,   whizzz, whizzzz

And sometimes if morale is low, he plays some bangin' tunes.

They dance   dance   dance
dance   dance   dance   dance   dance   dance
dance   dance   dance   dance

Days pass and soon the warehouse is all theirs.

They make sure that everyone has plenty of rest, and have enough breaks to eat and cry and share stories!

They make sure that everyone is paid and paid well!

They rip up the rules on the wall and write their own!

They rip the old sign and bring out their new:

> *WAREHOUSE RULES*
>
> 1. *Take Care of Each Other.*
>
> 2. *Take Care of This Space*
>
> 3. *Make Sure You Take Breaks*
>
> 4. *Be Generous*
>
> 5. *Be Welcoming*
>
> 6. *Have Fun!*
>
> 7. *Stay Hydrated*

They decide that this warehouse could be so much more than a warehouse!

It can be a community space with a community garden where they grow their own food.

It can be a space for art and crafts that everyone can use.

It can be a space for discovery and technology that is life changing for all.

And best of all, it's all free to use because everyone joins in.

Everyone gives a little and takes a little.

Everyone shares all the jobs.

The fun ones and the not-so-fun ones.

People still get their packages full of thoughtful gifts and stationery for school and novelty fashion items.

People still get their packages full of escapism and provoking thoughts and useless impulse purchases.

But this time the stickers, stackers and stampers do all the work themselves.

So sometimes the packages are a bit late but that's OK.

They don't have anyone shouting at them or tracking them or calling them by a number.

Because they share all the work, sometimes a stamper stacked, or a sticker stamped.

Stick, stamp, stack, stack, stamp, stick

They say that before the day the stampers united, no one believed that it was possible. No one believed that you could move how you wanted, in the rhythm that you wanted, at the pace that you needed.

But now . . .

 Stamp, stick, stamp,   stack, stack, stamp,   stick,stick,stack,stick

Thanks to the day the stampers united . . .

(and the stickers!)

(and the stackers!)

We all know it's possible.

A rush of movement and rhythm and colour.

An invitation to join in (or not).

A dazzling finish.

And The Name
for That Is...?
by Robert Softley Gale

Three actors at a minimum – an infinite maximum, perhaps! The actors playing **Nick** *and* **Ally** *can change every time a new drink is served, or not. I'd suggest all* **Nick**s *have the same costume, and likewise all* **Ally**s.

/ is used to denote interruption of the previous line.

Nick, *first person going in to coffee shop*

Ally, *person they're meeting*

Server

I've given almost no notes on blocking – it'd be obvious for **Nick** *and* **Ally** *to be sat at a table for the majority of the play but maybe doing something less obvious is more interesting. The* **Server** *floats between the counter, their table and the rest of the coffee shop – they should feel omnipresent.*

Anyone can play any of the parts – regardless of gender, race, disability, etc. If you think that the actors should mimic the changing impairments as they acquire them, then I think you might have missed the point. Proceed at own risk.

Serv So, we're in a Starbucks, which is a bloody awful place to set a piece of theatre. I'm telling you where we are because a) we haven't got the budget for the licence to use their logo and b) some folk here tonight might be blind, or visually impaired, so a logo wouldn't be much help to them anyway.

I work here. Don't judge me – I don't support the big corporate killing machine any more than other folk my age but it's flexible and it allows me to do this side hustle. I like helping people, you see – not just by bringing them their coffee but also by letting them see things in new ways. It's a gift that I've got – a talent. Here, let me show you.

Nick *enters, with book under their arm, and approaches the counter.*

Server Can I . . . what can I get you?

Nick A grande mocha with two pumps peppermint and hold the blah blah blah.

Server Nice. And the name for that is . . .?

Nick Nick.

Server N I C?

Nick K – yep

Server Got you. That'll be . . . a ridiculous amount. Just tap here.

Nick No worries.

Server (*noticing book*) Good read?

Nick Yeh, it is thanks. It's for uni – it's really got me thinking about /

Server Great. I'll bring your drink right over.

Nick It's fine – I can just wait /

Server No, no – we'll bring it to you. We're here to help folk in wheelchairs.

Nick   Folk in . . . what now?

Server   Just take a seat . . . I mean, a table. Just go to a table. We'll be right over.

Nick   Eemm. (*Heads towards a table.*)

Ally *enters, scans the place and spots* **Nick**.

Ally   Hi, are you, emmm . . .?

Nick   Nick – yeh, Nick – you're Ally, yeh?

Ally   Yeh – hi – nice to /

Nick   Yeh, you too. Yeh.

Ally   So, is this something you do quite a lot?

Nick   Drink coffee? Yeh!

Ally   Meet folk. For dates.

Nick   I've been on a few . . . You see, honestly there's no simple way to answer that question. If I say 'loads' I sound like a desperate saddo who nobody wants. If I say no then I'm clearly a loner who needs to get out more.

Ally   Whereas by explaining all of your inner thoughts you just sound . . . really intense.

Nick   OK, fair.

Ally   Look, I don't mean to be . . . rude. But I didn't realise when we were chatting that you were /

Nick   That I was in a /

Ally   Well, yeh! I mean it's absolutely fine. You're totally allowed to only say what you want to online, but . . .

Nick   Look, I'm going to be completely honest with you.

Ally   Appreciated.

Nick   I don't really know what you're seeing. The guy who served me – he suggested I was in . . . a wheelchair?

Ally   This is news to you?

Nick   Yes!

Ally   You're telling me you're not in a wheelchair?

Nick   No!!

Ally   Hold on – back up for a moment. So you /

Nick   I've got no idea what is going on here.

Ally   Look, this is too weird. I'm – no offence – you seem lovely but I'm off.

She leaves. She returns.

The doors are locked!

Nick   What? They're /

Ally   Locked. They're fucking locked. We're stuck in here. Did you set this up? Was this your idea?

Nick   What?

Ally   You and your disabled friends got some weird, twisted Saw movie fantasy?

Nick   I've been really clear – I'M NOT DISABLED!

Server   Hi. So I couldn't help but overhear – you both sound a little harassed.

Ally   We're stuck in here. The doors are bloody locked!

Server   Ah yes – that.

Nick   'That'?!

Server   Don't be too worried – I just find it helps to give people a wee bit of focus. Let's try a little exercise – a wee game. What we're going to do might be a bit scary for the two of you, or for anyone else watching

Ally   / Who the hell is watching?

Server   Other customers. Folk out there. I don't know. We're going to delve into matters that a lot of people would rather avoid talking about. My point is it should make you uncomfortable – if it doesn't scare you, you're not doing it right.

Nick, I saw from the book you're reading that you want to learn about disability – about disabled people and their perspective of the world.

Nick   It's for a course at uni /

Server   So you could just read about it – get a very academic perspective of the subject. Or . . . you could learn through experience. You could gain insight first hand.

Nick   How on earth do . . .

Server   / Humour me! (*To* **Ally**.) What if he was? What if he did use a wheelchair?

Ally   What? I . . . that's a ridiculous question!

Server   Maybe just go with it – for a bit. I mean you almost walked out on a guy just because he's disabled.

Ally   That's . . . I . . . no!

Server   Go with it – both of you. It might 'unlock' something.

Nick (*unsure*)   It really isn't a ridiculous question. [seeking the server's approval that he's going in the right direction] You've seen my face – we've chatted lots online – I could be in a wheelchair.

Ally   Eh – you are.

Nick   In your eyes.

Server   But he's asking you, seriously, would it make a difference to you? To how you see him?

Ally   Of course it wouldn't!

Nick   Not great at lying, are you? Your mouth's saying one thing but your face is saying something very different.

Ally   Well, it'd be a challenge – wouldn't it? It'd be a situation that we'd need to manage.

Nick   How so?

Ally   Well, if we're out and about, I'd need to push you up hills, wouldn't I? Which would be totally fine – of course it would. It's just . . . if a place wasn't accessible – if it didn't have a ramp and you couldn't get in, would that mean I couldn't go in either?

Nick   If you were a decent human being you probably wouldn't want to go in.

Ally   Ouch!

Nick   If a pub said NO BLACK PEOPLE and you went in, you'd be siding with racists, wouldn't you?

Ally   Well, yeh, I would.

Nick   So how is this different?

Ally   A pub wouldn't be allowed to say NO BLACKS. Not having a ramp is different.

Nick   Why? Just because it's about money – 'they can't afford to make it accessible so that's OK'?

Bollocks. Discrimination is discrimination – end of.

Ally   Calm down, would you? Why are you now the font of all disability knowledge anyway?

Nick   I . . . well I . . . honestly I've got no idea.

Server   Do you like the mocha syrup? Not bad, eh? And it's got a wee kick to it. Maybe that's where these ideas are coming from.

Ally   Oh come on!

Server   Some folk thought vaccines could implant GPS chips. So why can't a frappe syrup give you knowledge?

Ally   What about sex?

Nick   Wow, wow, wow, wow – slow down!

Ally   It's always at the back of your mind when you see a guy in a wheelchair. Can they . . .?

Nick   Maybe in your mind.

Ally   Not so cocky now, are you? Everyone's so progressive and 'right on' now and we all know sex is about a lot more than – well – the mechanics. But it's alright to wonder, how do disabled people do it?

Pause.

(*To* **Nick** *– enjoying his discomfort.*) So can you? Get . . .?

Nick   I bloody hope so!! Hold on a sec. (*Closes his eyes – beat.*) Yep, yes I can.

Ally   Eeww – were you just imagining . . .? Actually, I don't want to know!

Nick   So disabled people can be sexual beings as long as they don't rub it in your face? They should just keep it to themselves?

Ally   That isn't what I'm saying. It's just – I don't want to say the wrong thing – ask the wrong question.

Nick   Avoiding the subject altogether doesn't help anyone. Disabled people get treated as though they're children – don't mention the complex and messy stuff so we can pretend it doesn't happen.

Ally   OK, alright – I'll challenge myself with this. I mean, I reckon I'm pretty progressive so saying this shouldn't be – isn't – difficult. (*Deep breath.*) Disabled people have . . . relationships, yes – of course they do. But you're going to be limited, aren't you?

Nick Is this you not saying the wrong thing? Geez!

Ally Give me a chance, Nick! I'm trying to be honest about where I'm at.

Nick OK – that's fair. I mean, sure, when it comes to a physical relationship I – as a guy in a wheelchair – might not be able to flip you around and do handstands or anything like that. But my imagination isn't limited, is it? And I suppose places like these are great.

Ally Explain.

Nick Well, if two folk our age disappeared in to the toilet then folk would think something very dodgy was going on. But in here – every branch has an accessible toilet – and if you were helping me to get in there, well . . .

Ally Dirty bastard!

Nick Just saying!

Ally Going out with someone in a wheelchair. I mean it'd be tricky at times but there's no way it'd be a deal breaker for me. I'm progressive! This is all just stupid.

Server Drinks not quite what you were looking for?

Nick We don't know what it is you want from us!

Ally (*to* **Nick**) You're the one with the book! You're the one looking for answers!

Server You've got to work together. Here, come with me. I've another syrup for you to try.

Nick *goes to the counter.*

Nick (*returning to the table*) So the server has said to try these.

Ally (*gulping down*) Tastes great but, emm, you're getting fuzzy.

Nick What was that?

Ally I can only make out a rough outline of you /

Nick   And my hearing has gone – a lot. Everything sounds – really strange.

Ally   Would you stop shouting, please! So you're deaf and I'm . . . blind?

Nick   Not completely – not completely blind or deaf. I can still hear you . . . if I really try.

Ally   So I'm beginning to get this. The drinks are giving us the experience . . . or the appearance of having different impairments. It's some weird sort of body-swap with a disabled person kind of thing.

Nick   Yeh, something like that.

Ally   Is it permanent? Is this forever? I couldn't be blind – I just couldn't. Not seeing what my friends look like – what my family look like.

Nick   Calm down. The wheelchair didn't stay for me, did it? So I don't think any of this lasts.

Ally   So – right – we learn our lesson then get on with our lives.

Nick   But this one's a bit strange. It's like someone has hit a switch and suddenly I'm cut o – I can't hear what's going on. I'm on my own.

Ally   I think, to be honest, that I'd rather be in a wheelchair.

Nick   But are we compatible like this? The wheelchair sitch was difficult because it came with a power imbalance.

Ally   Potentially.

Nick   But if I'm deaf and you're blind it could be quite handy. You don't know which direction to go in when we're walking down the street so you can take my arm and I can guide you.

Ally   And you maybe can't hear traffic so you don't know when it's safe to cross the road. I can help with that.

Pause.

Nick   That's shit.

Ally   Why?

Nick   Deaf folk cross the street all the time without being hit by cars. They just look out for danger.

Ally   Oh yeh. I'd hate this though – not being able to look in to the eyes of someone you fancy and say 'You look hot tonight'. Not really knowing if they do look hot tonight!

Nick   If you've never had something, do you miss it?

Ally   I . . . 've no idea.

Nick   Like if you've never had sight, would you be that annoyed really at not being able to see?

Ally   But you know what 'seeing' is – you know that there's a world around you waiting to be seen. Unless you've never spoken to a sighted person in your life, you would know how other people have described the things that they've seen.

Nick   You might not know how hot I look. But you'd know that I smell sexy.

Ally   That stuff you're wearing smells like aftershave your mum put in your Christmas stocking.

Nick   Is being that nasty really necessary? Does it help us with this . . . situation? No! Zip it!

(*Clears throat.*) It could be romantic, couldn't it? Laying in the grass, reading books to one another /

Ally   I couldn't read a book unless the font was massive. And you couldn't hear what I was saying.

Nick   Come on – meet me half way. We could be a sweet couple!

Ally   Why? In what way is dependency 'sweet'? You're just trying to overcompensate by finding positivity in something that isn't. Being blind isn't a 'good' thing. Relying on someone isn't 'sweet'. I certainly never want to be dependent on anyone.

Nick   Ablism.

Ally   Eh?

Nick   You just can't help it. You've got this default view of disabled people as being inferior or 'less than'.

Ally   I'm not an . . . ableist. Or whatever you called it. Everyone's the same – we're all equal.

Nick   Except we're not – if we were we wouldn't be learning from these 'experiences'!

Ally   OK, not 'the same' – but we are all equal. We are!

Nick   I've honestly got no idea what that even means. We're all equal – we're all different – the words stop meaning anything at all after a while.

Ally   Such bollocks!

Nick   So are you really so against the idea of being dependent on someone else? Is that really so scary for you?

Ally   I'm not against anything. I just want to know I'm secure – that I don't need to rely on someone else.

Nick   Sounds pretty lonely.

Server   Some more drinks?

Ally *and* **Nick**   Yes!

Nick   Look, we're really trying here – we're doing our best to work out . . . whatever it is you want us to work out. Can you give us a hint?

Server   You're not doing this for me – you're doing it for yourselves.

Ally *and* **Nick**   Ehh?

Server   Please – just try these.

They both drink.

Ally   So what've we got now?

Nick   Sounds like something my mum would say! 'What's he got?' 'What's wrong with him?' 'What's the name for that?'

Ally   Are you talking about Nick's mum or Nick plus magic syrup's mum? Like, with the disability or . . .?

Nick   Yes – with it! Imaginary mum!

Ally   Your syrup-evoked mum doesn't understand disability?

Nick   Not even a smidge!

Ally   But she brought you up!

Nick   Means absolutely nothing. I get why you'd think it would but – honestly – zilch. You see, her approach to bringing up a disabled child was basically to be in denial. 'They're not disabled!' 'They're just a wee bit funny – nothing up with them!'

And it comes from a good place – I think. Treat a kid like everyone else and that's how they'll experience life.

Ally   But I'm guessing it doesn't really work like that?

Nick   Not in my experience, no. The thing is that I am different – there are these things that I just can't do. Wishing that fact away doesn't help.

Ally   All of this knowledge is . . . well, it's a lot. This syrup has got some power!

Nick   It really has! Like this thing called the Social Model of Disability. I was vaguely aware of it before – I'd heard about it – but now I feel like I know about it inside out.

Ally   I'm frightened to ask /

Nick   Well, basically it says that disabled people aren't 'held back' by their conditions, but instead by the barriers around them. You build stairs up to a building and no ramp – the stairs disabled me. You don't bother to give your staff Disability Equality Training, their patronising attitudes disable me.

But even this doesn't answer everything. Like when I was talking about my mum earlier, the Social Model is right up her street!! And yet I'm still disabled – I still find so many things difficult.

Ally   It's it's all just a bit right on?

Nick   'Right on' – 'PC' – terms that used to call people out have now just become . . . weapons. I can just shut down almost any argument you make without giving a counter-argument – without actually engaging with what you're saying at all. I just have to call you 'one of the PC brigade'.

Ally   Am I going to get an answer?

Nick   To?

Ally   What are our impairments now?

Nick   Hmmm, that's better. So you seem to be jerking a bit and your speech is slurred and I – well I'm in a wheelchair and my bones seem to be more visible.

Ally   Brittle bones. You've got a condition /

Nick   / Impairment

Ally   Aye – where a pretty minor fall or any impact can cause your bones to break.

Nick   Ouch!

Ally   I don't know which of these I'd rather have, to be honest.

Nick   Are there any disabilities you'd want to have?

Ally   I . . . I don't know. It's strange – we all joke about wanting to be the opposite gender for a day or two – peeing without having to sit down is the dream, isn't it? We even can see how being a different race could give you an advantage, or at least another view. But disability is different.

Nick   Is it?

Ally   No one says 'I really want to be disabled', do they?

Nick   Some folk have chosen to amputate their own legs. Nothing wrong with them – no medical issues or anything.

Ally   They just choose to use a wheelchair?

Nick   According to what I've read at uni, yeh. It's usually folk in America /

Ally   No surprise there!

Nick   They feel more like their 'authentic selves' when they have an impairment.

Ally   That just gives me the total ick.

Nick   Me too if I'm honest. But giving you or me the ick isn't a good enough reason to ban something.

Ally   Even if you could ban it.

Nick   You see, no one envies someone because they're disabled. Or, put it another way, no one has ever been expecting a baby and said 'I really hope they're born disabled'.

Ally   Deaf parents have. Some deaf people want to have deaf kids so their entire family can live in the same world.

Nick   That's just sick – wanting your children to be disabled.

Ally   Is it? Wouldn't you want to be able to communicate with your kids?

Nick   Yeh but /

Ally   If you couldn't – if you were deaf and you used sign language but your kids didn't, how would you build a relationship with them?

Nick   Yeh – I get that. But wanting to chat to your children in sign language and wishing they were deaf are two really different things.

Ally   Some deaf people don't see themselves as being disabled – they just use a different language from the rest of us. And along with that language comes a different experience of the world, and a different culture

Nick   Still though. It doesn't sit right.

Ally   Neither do we – with these drinks. Me with cerebral palsy and you with brittle bones. That's just never going to work. I jerk about and spasm quite a lot – uncontrollably. I'm strong – I might not be accurate but my muscles can pack a punch.

Nick   And my bones break with the least amount of force. I'm delicate.

Ally   Exactly.

Nick   So you could just be giving me a hug and a spasm could hit you and snap – my arm gets broken.

Ally   It's not on purpose!

Nick   I'm sure that'll make a big difference when I'm in a cast!

Ally   Fair

Pause.

Nick   Your jerky hands could be, emm, quite useful . . .

Ally   What?

Nick   You know! (*Wanking gesture.*)

Ally   You sick prat!

Nick   My pal's dad got Parkinson's years ago, which is obviously a terrible condition. Like really hard. But I swear that as the months passed and his hand tremors got worse, you could see his wife getting happier!

Ally   What did she have to be happy about?

Nick   She was married to a guy who had hands that were like a sex toy – no batteries required!

Ally   You are a sick, sick /

Nick   Nah! But wait, shouldn't we be – how do you put it? 'Inhabiting' these impairments? Just to see what they feel like?

Ally   So I should slur my speech and act like I've got CP? Are you a big star looking for an Oscar?

Server   While we're paused, can I just add that if you ever get the urge to 'pretend' to be disabled, please do it in private. Do not – I repeat do not – inflict other people with your mockery.

Nick   But I thought we were actors.

Server   Would you pretend to be a character of another race?

Nick   Actually no – ignore that idea.

Ally   Thank gawd! So brittle bones and cerebral palsy – a bad combo, right?

Nick   Yeh I reckon. Are we any closer to getting out of this place?

Server   You're so fixated on getting away. Just enjoy the lesson a bit more.

One more drink?

Ally   Fine. Yes!

Server   Coming right up.

They drink.

Ally   The world – how I'm perceiving it – just seems to be a little bit different.

Nick   Your vision? We've done blind already!

Ally   No – not my vision – my perception. Things in this place just don't make sense in the way they did a few minutes ago.

Nick   You're neurodiverse!

Ally   Ha! Well, that sounds pretty typical! Most ND folk that I know didn't know that they were neurodiverse for ages – they just know they're not like other people.

Nick   We spend our lives comparing ourselves to each other – it's fecking weird.

Ally   I think it's unavoidable. We need reference points – it'd be too unsettling to just float along.

Nick   So am I right? Are you neurodiverse?

Ally   Yeh – possibly. Aren't you?

Nick   No, I don't think I am.

Ally   And that's got to be difficult. A neurodiverse person dating someone who sees the world in a really typical way.

Nick   It'd bring challenges, yeh.

Ally   We're just going to fight loads – misunderstand each other all the time.

Nick   Maybe – or maybe in trying to communicate – in being forced to make an effort – you find something more?

Ally   Sounds like hard work!

Nick   If you're looking to avoid hard work, stay single! The thing we all claim to be looking for is connection – finding someone who makes us feel just a tiny bit less alone in the world. What if that person – for you – has a non-neurotypical brain? What if their way of seeing the world forces them – forces both of you – to ask questions that you'd otherwise make presumptions about? What if that kind of relationship is healthier?

Ally   What if it's an absolute nightmare?

Nick It's probably both.

Do you think it'd be easier for someone who is neurodiverse to go out with another neurodiverse person?

Ally Isn't that a bit patronising? 'Just you all stick to your own tribe' – saves the rest of us from having to adapt or evolve!

Nick OK – point taken. But what if it's easier for the person though? Does the individual really need to work and struggle for the benefit of the 'greater good'?

Ally Hashtag nosimplequestions?

Server We're closing up soon – can I get you both one last drink?

Ally Sure!

They drink.

Pause.

I'm sure it'll kick in soon . . .

Nick Starbucks, eh?! I mean sure, they've been found to use slave labour to produce their coffee, but if you're a Gold member you get free syrup, so c'mon!

Ally You know, Nick – sometimes . . . usually, in fact – silence is better than just talking absolute shite for the sake of it.

Nick Ally! It's . . . there's no easy way to say this. It's terminal.

Ally You're dying?

Nick No – you are!

Ally Great! At least it'll get me out of here!

Nick It'd be really difficult – especially at our age. Dating someone when you know they haven't got long to live.

Ally   Is cancer a disability? I never really thought of it that way.

Nick   It can be – depends how much it impacts your day-to-day life. But I never said you had cancer.

Ally   What have I got?

Nick   It doesn't matter. What does matter is that you've got six months to live.

Ally   I've got zero energy – I just feel incredibly tired and incredibly sick. This is shit.

Nick   I'm here for you – through the treatment.

Ally   Well that's . . . great. So we grasp every moment. Tick off everything on our bucket list. Be present!

Nick   Yeh. We'll travel to places and experience the world together – we'll really get to know each other.

Ally   But – I mean, yeh, sure – but why? What would be the point? 'Let's get to know each other so you can then lose me and be consumed by grief?' I just can't imagine that as being a functional relationship – as being a functional way to live.

Nick   So we just stay friends?

Ally   Same issue really. We'd still be getting closer to each other knowing that this looming endpoint was hurtling towards you.

Nick   Imagine knowing that each time you kissed, each time you had sex, could be your last?

Ally   Maybe that is how we should kiss. Knowing it could be our last.

There. Is that the lesson? Can we get the hell out now?

Server   Kiss and it'll all be fixed? He's not a frog and no one's being turned in to a prince tonight!

Ally   We've tried everything!

Server   You really think this is all just about finding a bit of carpe diem? 'Live in the moment.' 'Be present.' This isn't an inspirational Facebook meme.

Nick   Facebook? Are you forty?

Server   Ha ha!

Ally   We've done everything we've been asked to. We've explored these situations.

Nick   If we're not giving you the right answer, it isn't our fault!

Server   I don't need an answer – wrong or right.

Ally   Well, what then?

Server   I just wanted to open up a tiny bit of a possibility. For you to see things from slightly different perspectives.

That's what your book was all about, wasn't it? Gaining new perspectives.

I'm not naive. I'm not fooling myself that you'll leave here tonight and the next disabled person you meet will instantly be 'the one for you'. But maybe these chats that you two have had will allow you to look twice – to wonder 'what if?'

The perfect match – for most folk – doesn't really exist. Even a good match is pretty difficult to find. But if you're passing over folk because they speak a bit funny or because they can't see, then you're potentially missing out on something. Maybe you're missing out on the good stuff?

Ally   OK – we promise not to be so judgemental. To see beyond the surface.

Server   Nah – don't see beyond it. See the surface – *and* what's beneath. See all of it. It's all part of the big picture.

Anyway, lesson over, spell broken. The doors are open. You're free to go.

Nick   What do we owe you for the drinks?

Server   You're a Gold member, yeh? So the syrups are free – but the lessons are priceless.

Ally   Oh geesus – I think I can feel that last one coming back up!

Server   See you later!

Nick   Ally, I – I really enjoyed meeting you. It was . . . really weird – but good!

Ally   Yeh, same.

Nick   I'd like to /

Ally   Yeh, we can do it again. Although maybe leave the books at home next time!

Server   So – there we go. Take whatever lessons you want from this – diversity is a good thing, don't be afraid of asking the wrong questions when it comes to disabled people, and yes they do have sex! Or maybe the lesson is as simple as trying a new syrup next time you go for a coffee?

Nick/Ally   Oh please!

Blackout.

Thanks for Nothing
by The PappyShow
with Lewis Hetherington

Hello there!

Before we begin . . .

This is a quick letter for you, the person (or people) who will be leading the process on *Thanks for Nothing*. Leading a creative process is such a wonderful job. It's such a difficult job. Thank you for taking it on and making this opportunity for your group!

Everything that follows is for you to use however you want. Read it through first, the whole thing. It will probably not make total sense at first – that's ok. It will probably never make TOTAL sense, as it's all about suggestions, nudges and paths for you to follow, however you want to follow.

We have included a whole process leading you all the way up to making a show. But if you don't have time or resources for that, you can do it your way, pick out some of the ideas that would work for your group and go from there.

Once you've read the whole thing, you can think about how you share it with your group. Perhaps you want to just give them everything as it is? Or perhaps you might choose to offer it bit by bit, if that would make it more accessible and fun? Perhaps you share this letter with them too? It's up to you!

We at The PappyShow are all about collaboration, creating a space where everyone can contribute the way they want to. Someone needs to make that happen though, and that's you!

This process, like any artistic process, will take people into surprising and unexpected corners of their internal emotional landscape, and it's your job to make sure everyone feels safe and secure.

People will be asked to share stories from their lives, but it's really important that people know there is no pressure to share anything they don't want to share. Everyone should only say things they are happy for the group to hear, and potentially include in the show.

Sometimes, when people are asked to share something personal in a rehearsal room they think they have to share something shocking or surprising. Perhaps this is because people often fear that they are not enough, that they must give more, they must 'dig deep' . . . But this is not the case. Everyone is enough with what they have to give.

In our experience, it is often the little things, the details, the tiny quirks, the domestic rituals, that feel most interesting, surprising and nourishing for us as makers, and for our audiences. If we set an atmosphere of curiosity, of attention and interest, we can find magic in the everyday.

So remind people to take care of themselves and each other. We are not looking to empty people out, but to fill them up. This goes for you too of course! Make sure you take care of yourself! Be sure to think about the people you will go to, to share your thoughts and feelings. Who are the people around you who could be a mentor, a supporting hand, a brain to bounce ideas around with?

Allow yourself to remain open to surprises and discoveries along the way. Try to remember that what we have offered is a series of diving boards; it's up to you how you jump into the water. It is not a strict list which you must laboriously get through; it's an invitation to create, to think, to play.

ALSO. Though we have not given you a *play*, we want you to **play**! If things feel difficult, how can you make it easier? You will all have to work hard, but never in a way that gets in the way of sparking joy.

We are so excited that you are joining The PappyShow team. We can't wait to see what you've made, to see all the things you're thankful for and how you celebrated that.

You're going to be amazing, we just know it.

The PappyShow.

CONTENTS

1. A LETTER TO EVERYONE

Dear new friends,

Hello! Thanks so much for choosing to work on this piece!

First of all – congratulations! You already have everything you need to make this show! You, the people in this room, are enough. Your ideas, your bodies, and your hopes and fears are everything we need to make this happen.

We, The PappyShow, are always so delighted to welcome new people into the family! We think that the more people, the more ideas, the more energy in a room, means the more exciting, rewarding and eye opening working together will be.

We encourage you to think about that when you're putting together this piece – who else might be interesting to include? Who might bring something into the mix which isn't there at the moment? Who is not in the room who might have something to add? Who can you invite in to work with you?

It is hard to make a performance. It can feel overwhelming. But the thing to do is to trust the process you have here. Trust yourselves and each other. You've got this. Some of the things we ask you to do might seem strange at first; it might not be immediately clear how they are helping you make a show. But we PROMISE you that getting to know each other, creating an atmosphere where everyone feels safe and happy, like they can be themselves, is VITAL. You can't do anything truly creative without taking care of that.

The show you make will contain only a glimmer of all you experience together, and that's ok! The thing to do is to listen, be kind, take care and give whatever you can give. No more or less; make sure you look after yourself and contribute in the way that is right for you.

If you have a magical, brave and silly time as you are creating, then that will shine through in the performance, and the people in your audience will be held by that.

–

This process is called *Thanks for Nothing*. It's our little joke because we haven't given you a script. But also it's because we wanted to encourage you to explore the notion of being thankful, being grateful.

We did some silly, moving and challenging sessions developing this piece. At first it seemed simple, asking what we are grateful for (puppies, ice cream, daffodils!), what we are not grateful for (smelly trains, wet feet, rude people), and how we show we are thankful (a smile, a card, a bunch of flowers).

But as time went on, as we waded out deeper into the water, it became increasingly complicated, and increasingly beautiful. Perhaps especially now, living through a global pandemic, a climate breakdown, with so many people suffering and struggling, it is a strange time to think about being thankful.

When you start to think of the things that you are *really*, *truly* thankful for, the people, the family, the friends, the natural world – how do you begin to express that? How do you begin to describe that? It can feel massive . . .

As filmmaker David Lynch says, you have to wade out deep if you want to catch a big fish.

That's why this is a process, you won't find all the answers, and you're not supposed to. It's the journey to the depths of the ocean and back. It's about finding some ways to think about and feel gratitude, which will maybe stay with you a long time. Maybe when we are no longer in this room together, when we are miles apart, when our bodies have aged and the world has shifted under our feet, something of what we taught each other will stay with us.

So! Let's get going! Together! We can't wait to hear all about what you get up to!

Lots of love,

The PappyShow.

Photo credits from left to right clockwise: Helen Murray, Alex Brenner, Cesar Mota

2. WHAT WE ARE OFFERING YOU

CREATING: 15 provocations

These are a mix of questions and challenges and ideas to get you all creating things as a group. They are curious, playful, and most importantly very open in terms of how you can respond and react. We think each provocation should have its own session. You can do them in the order we have suggested or you can change to a different order. You can let the group make choices about the order if that feels right.

SHAPING: A toolkit

These are a series of techniques to help you create a curious and productive space and then to help you shape and choose your material.

Some are big ideas that you will want to use all the time. Others are more of a one off to use occasionally . . .

SHARING: A path to performance

Photo credit: Alessandra Davison

Each performance of *Thanks for Nothing* will be very different. It will be shaped and formed by YOUR company, by the stories and lives and hopes and fears of the people in the room who are making it.

But we have created a pathway which you can follow. To help you create material, to help you shape material and to help you finalise the performance.

The path is there if you need it – but don't be afraid to wonder off, take a detour, change direction entirely. You can always return to the path when you need to.

This performance can be anything. You can use any form that fits your group. There are a few things that every show will include (more on that later), but other than that, follow your instincts. A film, a fashion show, a cabaret, an exhibition. Whatever works for you!

3. CREATING

Here is a list of our 15 invitations to get creating, and a suggested order. You might want to change that order though! That's up to you. You might want to decide together, or pull them out of a hat.

Bear in mind that some of them need preparation, some require people to bring something personal along, or materials to work with so the group leaders will need to gather that. BUT! When you are getting materials – use what you have! It should not cost a lot to you, or the planet! Source what you can find – that's enough. Make simple and bold choices. Maybe some people might be up for helping you find things? Maybe that is a way to include other voices?

Anyway! Here are the invitations in brief:

15 invitations to create

1. Thank you for being here.

2. Thank you for watching.

3. Thank you for being a monster.

4. Thank you for listening.

5. Thank you for the world you've given us!?!!?!?! It's a mess!

6. Thank you for sharing.

7. Thank you for all the big things and the little things and everything in between and the weird stuff which we don't even know why it's important yet but it is and also the things that maybe are small and you barely notice but they are there and they do make a difference.

8. Thank you for making an effort.

9. Thank you for the dancing.

10. Thank you for trying.

11. Thank you for making it mean something.

12. Thank you for this old pile of rubbish.

13. Thank you for joining me in the future.

14. Thank you for writing to me.

15. Thank you for coming to our show but we think you need to understand a bit better what we've been up to, because we can't fit it all into the show but we can let you know a little bit more about it.

THOSE INVITATIONS IN MORE DETAIL . . .

1. Thank you for being here

This is a chance to get to know each other. To be playful, silly and connect with one another.

Perhaps you start this session by reading out the letter from The PappyShow!

Play games, get people moving and interacting with one another. Ball games, dancing games, moving around games. Playful games.

Then we suggest you draw up an agreement of what you want the room to be like. Have a discussion. What are the things that you expect of each other? Stick it up on the wall or somewhere you can always see it.

Explore the ways we can say thank you. Perhaps you go round in a circle, or make big lists of all the things you are thankful for.

And then the things you are NOT thankful for.

Ask people to close their eyes and think on their own what it feels like when someone does something kind to you? How does it feel in your body and imagination? What colour is it? What does it smell like? What animal is it? What type of weather is it?

Get people, maybe in small groups, to use their bodies to make frozen pictures of someone being grateful, make it as ridiculous and silly as possible.

Do it again with people being ungrateful.

Perhaps you end the session by writing a letter to yourselves in the future, to ask questions, to share what you are thinking so far, who is all there, what you're excited about!

You can then open this just before you do your first performance.

WHY DO THIS?

To start building this atmosphere we've talked about, where everyone feels welcome, relaxed and inspired. To dip your toes in the waters of our theme of being thankful.

2. Thank you for watching

In this session you will make a trailer for the show you have not yet made.

Perhaps you start this session by watching some trailers for movies, maybe ones which feel really different in tone and style and content?

In small groups you create short trailers, live or recorded, for this show *Thanks for Nothing*, which you have not made yet. What might it include? What might it look like? What might people think of it?

The only rule is to be really confident about how you present it. You can be absolutely sure that *your* version is the true version, and that it was a brilliant show!

WHY DO THIS?

To let your imaginations run wild about what this show could possibly be? It's a chance to devise a piece of performance in a very low-risk way; it's just for you to share with each other for fun.

3. Thank you for being a monster

This is about trying to create a beast which would be perfect for showing gratitude.

Perhaps this session starts with images of beasts all over the room, from fact and fiction, with all their teeth and claws and googly eyes and purple fur and so on. All the peculiarities which make them a monster.

On a giant piece of paper on the floor you will start to write out things which would be useful if you are trying to show someone how grateful you are.

Then people will individually draw and design their own THANK YOU monsters. Give them names.

Then you will all come together to discuss and start to design one mega monster. Working collaboratively to uncover your ideas.

You will then construct the monster you designed together, out of rubbish, a kind of giant puppet, that you will bring to

Photo credit: Dan Weill

life. (Maybe if your group is big you might design and make a few monsters.)

Give the monster a name. How does it move? What sound does it make? How does it explore the world? How does it interact with people?

What does it look like if the thank you monster is not grateful, or is just pretending to be grateful? Can you take it out into the street?

WHY DO THIS?

To give us a chance to get physical, get moving, to visualise ideas around gratitude. To make sure we don't get stuck in everything being realistic and chatty. To approach the topic in a silly way.

4. Thank you for listening

This is about REALLY listening. Not just waiting for your turn to speak.

Perhaps you start this session by asking everyone to be silent for five minutes, and just hear whatever sounds there might be in the room. Just listen! What do you hear outside yourself? What do you hear inside yourself? Maybe you make the room feel nice with candles or bean bags for everyone to lie on.

Next, in pairs, take turns to speak. Partner A has to talk about themselves (where they live, what they like or don't like, what they hope for, what they are scared of, anything!) for five whole minutes and Partner B JUST listens. Then they swap over.

Then they make a list of all the things they can remember about the other person. Then everybody presents their partner back to the group, and talks about what they have just heard about them.

People have to create a self-portrait of their partner BUT it must not be a drawing. It can be a collection of objects, a poem, a piece of expressive movement. It does not have to be literal, but just show something of the spirit of that person you've heard about.

Perhaps you have a discussion about what it feels like to have to just TALK. And what it feels like to just LISTEN.

WHY DO THIS?

To really connect with each other, to get to know each other better and feel even more free to take risks. It also really makes sure everyone gets a chance to be heard.

5. Thank you for the world you've given us!?!!?!?! It's a mess!

As we know, there is a lot going on in the world today. A lot of it is messy, complicated and difficult. That's what we're going to look at today.

Perhaps you start this session with a newspaper, or a few. And invite people to choose a story which captures their attention, makes them think.

Through discussion, start to talk about all the ways in which adults have made a mess. All the things which young people are going to have to deal with. Think of a mix of things which are global, but also local. It's about climate change but it's also about the broken street lamps outside the school. It's about people not having enough food to eat, but it's also about the broken swings in the park which haven't been fixed in years.

Together as a group, you will write a manifesto! You're tired of being told by adults to tidy up after yourselves – it's time they tidied up after THEMSELVES!

Perhaps you watch some videos and examples of inspiring speakers and thinkers, TED talks, YouTube videos, from Malala or Beyoncé or the local lollipop man. These might inspire you to think about how you communicate your message.

Write your manifesto and then decide how you will perform it as a group.

WHY DO THIS?

Because the world is complicated at the moment, we are facing many huge challenges, so sometimes we don't feel grateful, we feel frustrated, we feel the weight of things which feel beyond our control. We need to talk about it.

6. Thanks for sharing

This session is about food! People need to bring along food that is important to them, if they can! Whatever it is, angel delight or pakora or homemade jam, they need to know in advance so they can bring it along.

Perhaps you start this session with a picnic basket on a blanket. Everyone sits around in a circle and you tell them you're going for a picnic.

First of all, where can you have your picnic? Can you get to the beach, the forest, an old ruined castle? Perhaps to the school playground? Or maybe you can't go anywhere and you have to change the room. Put blankets out on the floor, put on a soundtrack of tweeting birds and a babbling brook. Maybe bring your sunglasses, your camping chair. Or close your eyes and imagine it! Be sure to get some photos of yourselves on your lovely picnic!

Lay out the picnic that people have brought and make it look beautiful, not fancy and posh necessarily, just beautiful. Before you eat you will hear each person tell their story of why their food is important – what is the story of why they brought that food?

If there are lots of you, you could break it into stages, something like this:

1. Set the picnic
2. Hear some stories
3. Have first round of eating
4. More stories
5. Have second round of eating
6. Final stories.

WHY DO THIS?

Eating together is an ancient and beautiful way of building relationships. It gives us a chance to fill ourselves up together, to nourish one another with food, stories and company. It gives a chance for stories to emerge in a really organic way.

7. Thank you for all the big things and the little things and everything in between and the weird stuff which I don't even know why it's important yet but it is and the things that maybe are small and you barely notice but they are there and they do make a difference.

This is about really diving deep, down into the depths of the ocean. The ocean of gratitude. Really thinking imaginatively about the theme.

Perhaps this session starts with a huge sheet of paper on the floor, and some wonderful watery music playing. With all sorts of odds and ends of junk and crafty material . . .

The whole company are going to fill this ocean. They are going to show all the creatures and life forms, an octopus of indecision, a whale of kindness, a bad attitude barracuda . . . But people don't have to explain, you are just together creating one amazing huge picture of an ocean. An ocean of gratitude.

How does this become a performance? How do we immerse an audience in this? How do we make them FEEL like they are in this ocean themselves, exploring . . . ?

Perhaps you build the landscape of the bottom of the sea with whatever you have, chairs, tables, bags. Then you build the creatures from whatever else is left lying around. Perhaps the group splits in half and takes it in turns to be deep sea divers and creatures. The deep sea divers have to swim the depths and report back what they saw . . . .

WHY DO THIS?

The ocean of gratitude is a grounding idea for the whole piece. It reminds us that this exploration of being thankful is ongoing, mysterious and ever shifting, like the great wide sea. It also might give us some very cool design ideas for the show.

8. Thank you for making an effort

This is about acknowledging someone who is making a difference. It might be the person at the end of your street who grows vegetables, it might be Greta Thunberg or Marcus Rashford, it might be your big sister who is training to be a nurse.

Perhaps you start this session by putting up a picture of the person who you are grateful to for making an effort – you'd need to ask everyone in advance to bring their picture! If they forget they could draw it, or just write the name on a big piece of paper.

Have a look at these pictures like a gallery. Then let everyone briefly introduce the people and their stories.

As a group, decide on a couple of people who you think are really interesting; try to make it so that the handful of people you chose are very different in what they are doing and how they do it.

Each group is then asked to think about what they would do if they met that person. What would you say if they walked in that door right now? Prepare a little performance for what you would do – what would you say? How would you thank them? Is there any advice you would give them?

WHY DO THIS?

It's a way to think about the problems we face, but through the ways in which people are making the world better. It's another way to get to know each other better, and all the surprising and interesting things which other people are passionate about.

9. Thank you for the dancing

It's time to get those bodies moving!

Perhaps you can lay out a dancefloor, or get some lights and a disco ball, or some big speakers? Get a rail of disco costumes! Create an atmosphere!

In this session you will create a moment of dance for everyone to participate in. It will be a big joyful moment of celebration. Depending on the group it might be lots of steps and moves, or perhaps it is more free, but either way in this session you'll create some structure so everyone knows what they are doing in this moment of dance.

As a group you will choose one of the songs that will come out of 'Thank you for the Music' (we'll explain that later on). Choose something that felt really special and fun and that you think your audience will enjoy, and you will make your piece of dance out of that.

Photo credit: Cesar Mota

Maybe it's a song you can play and sing live if people in your group have those skills? Maybe you can bring someone else in to play along with you?

WHY DO THIS?

We at The PappyShow love moving, whatever that looks like for your body! It is a way to express ourselves without words, to say the things we don't know how to say, but just how they FEEL. It will also create some great moments of performance!

10. Thank you for trying

This is all about impossible tasks, things that can't be done but we're going to try them anyway.

Perhaps you start this session by having everyone stand around a mystery box, which is filled with impossible tasks. People go up one at a time to take a challenge out, read it aloud, and then the group has one minute (or more?) to try and do it. And you have to REALLY TRY. You have to take it seriously and do it.

Impossible tasks might be: Try to fly! (stay safe!); Try to move a chair with your mind; Try to catch a bit of air and put it in your pocket; Try to be four thousand years old; Try to do a dance to represent how we achieve world peace.

In groups, you write a task and give it to another group. Each group creates a small performance based on attempting the task they have been given. Everyone watches each other. Then, each group creates another mini-performance inspired by one of the performances they have seen. You can work out how to allocate it, but each group should respond to a performance that came out of a challenge they don't know about.

What happens if you have to do your performance over and over again until you're exhausted. What happens if everyone all learns the rules of one of the performances and you all do that as a group? One big performance repeated again and again . . . .

Think about the tokens you could give. Perhaps you think your dad deserves all the sun in the sky, so you fill a jar with gold foil. Perhaps you wish you could give your granny all the flowers in the world, so you could make a paper daisy everyday for a year and collect them in a box?

WHY DO THIS?

To explore the idea that some things are worth doing even if they are impossible, because of what we find out about ourselves along the way. And though we might not complete

Photo credit: Helen Murray

the task, we might achieve all sorts of other things along the
way, such as renewed hope, laughter, a deeper bond with
our friends, a new way of looking at the world . . .

11. Thank you for making it mean something.

This session is about creating your own ritual of thanks.

Perhaps you start this by standing in a circle and everyone turns to the person next to them and creates a high five/handshake to show thanks to each other.

What are the ways we say thank you? Do they feel like enough? When someone has done something amazing, how can we really show our appreciation?

In small groups, think of something you are all thankful for. Then create a small ritual that you can do to show you are thankful.

Perhaps you share examples of rituals, like someone receiving a medal, or a wedding which often feature many moments of ritual, or a prayer, or other ones from the group

Your ritual should have some movement, but that movement can be everyday, like a wave, a nod or smile or . . . there will maybe be a few words, or music, or objects, but it can be quite simple. It is something that can be done alone or together. Perhaps it can be done in different ways, depending on how you feel that day?

Teach each other your rituals.

WHY DO THIS?

One of the things we realised that makes gratitude complicated is because we often don't have many rituals to mark, not ones that feel special or specific . . . It's a chance to find how to feel thankful, to locate it, to create gestures to embody it.

12. Thank you for this pile of old rubbish

We're going to create something ridiculously beautiful from a big pile of rubbish.

Perhaps this session starts with a huge pile of rubbish and recycling in the room. All clean of course! Cardboard, paper, bed sheets, a broom handle, a broken linen basket. Only things which don't have a use anymore.

You are going to create a fashion show. Perhaps some of you will make outfits. Perhaps some of you will make the catwalk.

Perhaps you watch some amazing fashion shows as inspiration, from designers like Alexander McQueen or Iris Van Herpen to get some ideas for how to walk the catwalk! Perhaps you share some images from the Met gala of people in fantastic and interesting outfits for inspiration.

Everything you make will be from the pile of rubbish. You might have sellotape, string, staples and glue or other things to help hold bits together, but it must be made from rubbish.

Create your fashion show! Make a catwalk, choose your music; maybe you'll have someone describing the outfits! Have fun!

Maybe your fashion show includes outfits that will help you take that deep sea dive into the ocean of gratitude? Or maybe your fashion outfits will look like some of those strange beautiful beasts we saw in the deep . . . .

WHY DO THIS?

This is a great way for you to think about what your show will look like, what you might wear, what it would represent. It's a great way to celebrate that the joy of creativity is often about creating something seemingly from nothing.

13. Thank you for joining me in the future

This is about stepping into tomorrow! People will need to bring a suitcase, or a duffel bag, or something they can pack!

Perhaps start this with giving out tickets to 2050? That's where we are headed! Everyone will need a suitcase.

Ask people to think about what we need to take to the future. Individually people will make their own lists. It should include practical things like flippers and plant seeds, but also abstract things like hope, determination, playfulness.

People then have to choose objects which represent those things. You'll have to think hard about what object might represent hope, and why?

People share what is in their suitcase.

How do we make that into a moment of performance? In a way that is simple and direct.

WHY DO THIS?

As we have been looking at some of the difficult things in the world, it's really important we look forward to the future and the kind of world we might like to build and how we might do it.

14. Thank you for writing me a letter

As it sounds . . .

Perhaps you start this with a letter written to the group, from you, the group leader, to everybody in the room. Perhaps you thank them for their work so far! A letter is a good way to say thank you, and so that's what you're going to do.

There will be paper and stamps and envelopes for everyone. Bring in some materials for people to write, maybe colourful paper and pens. But maybe you'll just lay out blank sheets of white paper on the floor, enough for every member of the group.

People will take some time to think about who they want to write to. To say thank you for something. They will need to remember that these might be shared in the show.

You will all hear the letters together. Perhaps everyone will come up with three gestures, which represent their letter, could be literal or behavioural, or it could be abstract.

How can we make that a moment of performance? With movement, music, or costume?

These letters will be posted! So be sure to make copies as you might need them for the show.

WHY DO THIS?

It's a chance for people to reflect, in a very personal way, what they are thankful for. It is also a way to create text which you might use in your performance.

15. Thank you for coming to our show but we think you need to understand a bit better what we've been up to, because we can't fit it all into the show but we can let you know a little bit more about it!

This session is about thinking about what task you could get the audience to do, during the show, to make them think about being thankful, and to give them an insight into what it's been like for you.

Together you decide upon an exercise that you would like the audience to do. It needs to be simple, with very minimal or no equipment or preparation required.

Think about how the audience will feel when they come to see the show; they probably won't expect to have to get involved so you should perhaps be kind.

It might be very simple, you may ask them to close their eyes and think of something they are grateful for. Perhaps they will all shout out at once, really loud, something that they are not grateful for. Or perhaps they will tell the person next

Photo credit: Cesar Mota

to them something they are really really truly thankful for. Perhaps they learn one of the rituals for gratitude which you created?

WHY DO THIS?

We are all about process at The PappyShow so we want to share that with the audience too. Lots of people will not really know what goes on in this kind of creative process so this is a chance to give them a taste! We think it's really important to acknowledge how special it is that all these people, the company and the audience, are all together in a room and we should celebrate that! We should have a moment to look each other in the eye and say here we are! This moment is special!

4. SHAPING

CHECK-IN

Every session should begin with a check-in. A check-in is when you make a circle, and one by one you hear from every person, they say how they are feeling in that moment. Sometimes you might add other questions to get people thinking about certain topics, or to set a mood. What is your favourite place in the world? Tell us about a time you felt proud? Even when you feel like there isn't enough time to check in, that's actually the most important time to do it! People knowing they are welcome and they have a voice is always the key!

GET ON YOUR FEET!

Every session should have a moment of performance, maybe lots of moments of performance. Talking and thinking is great. But so is doing! Every time you perform you have a chance to get better at performing, find new things, build relationships, explore your voice and body. The more you share these moments of performance, the easier it will be to build your show.

THE KEEP

The keep is a part of a castle, the strongest and most fortified part of the castle. A tower where you keep things safe, the things you absolutely need.

At the end of every session, everyone will discuss which things will go into the Keep. It might be a line of text, a song, an image, an object, a piece of choreography . . . Or perhaps a full monologue or a scene that has been created.

It does not have to be something that EVERYONE totally agrees on, but it does have to be really important and significant to what has been happening in the room.

Maybe it's even a colour, or a material, or a shape? Maybe it's a design idea, a piece of set, a costume?

Not everything in the keep will go into the show, but it might!

Maybe your keep will be an old chest, maybe it will be a shoe box wrapped in gold paper that you keep somewhere really high, maybe it will be a battered old suitcase, maybe a pinboard on the wall.

THANK YOU FOR THE MUSIC

Over the course of your CREATING phase, every person will bring in a song which means a lot to them. Maybe that will be one person per session, or two, or maybe everyone will do it at the same session?

They will tell us why it is important to them, in detail. It doesn't have to be a long explanation but it has to be *specific*. It can't just be like 'this is a good tune'; each person has to

Photo credit: Alex Brenner

explain why this track has meaning for them. But of course, just what people feel safe and comfortable to share.

Once you have heard the story, you all dance to it together, with that story in mind. Or perhaps you all lie on the floor looking at the ceiling and listen to it if that feels more like the right thing to do . . .

It's up to you when you do this, as a warm-up, as a wind-down, or maybe it's different in each session?

Once you've heard all the tracks, you will as a group reflect on which one you'd like to create a dance section for.

Perhaps you'd like to include more songs? Maybe want to do a cover version of one of the other songs? Maybe you want to use them as the music to play as the audience comes in?

THE MULTIPLIER

As you create and play we want you to always think about THE MULTIPLIER.

This means that every time you share and create, you think about more than one element. Live performance is 3D! Maybe even 4D? Or 5D?

Each time you create, it's never just movement, or just text, or just design, because you will use THE MULTIPLIER.

If someone has written a beautiful letter, what could we do to enhance it? Change the lighting by turning the lights off and adding a single candle flame? Or perhaps someone could create some movement to accompany the letter, simple gestures which the rest of the company do in the background behind the person reading? Perhaps the person reading the letter has a costume made of hundreds of handwritten versions of the same letter?

It's up to you to try in the room. Don't be afraid to get it wrong – that's where the interesting stuff might happen! Take a risk, throw some things together which shouldn't work, and you might just find something truly unique and beautiful.

IN CASE OF EMERGENCY

Let the company know about this on day one. It's for that bit in the process when things get a bit stuck, or complicated, or you're just seeking new ideas. IT CAN ONLY BE USED ONCE!

It's a golden envelope that the group can decide to open in an emergency. If things feel tricky, or confusing. This is what is inside it.

Hello, everyone!

So you've opened the emergency envelope – good for you!

Perhaps things are feeling tricky, or sticky, but we promise, you are on track! Getting lost is ALWAYS part of the process.

What you're going to do now is put on a song, and you're going to dance like crazy. You have one minute to decide what the song is together.

Whatever it is, you dance, shake, boogie, jump.

And then you sit in a circle, and one by one you give the person next to you a compliment. You tell them something that you really like about them that you have seen during this process. It might be a quality they have. It might be an idea they have had in this process or a performance they have done.

It is not always an easy thing to do! But it is a magical thing. It can be very simple, but let it be very truthful.

Remember, everything you need to make a brilliant show is already here. It is you, and your stories.

5. SHARING

In this section we'll give you some thoughts on how to put together your performance – whatever that is going to look like!

These are really only guidelines. It is totally up to you! You know what you have created better than anyone else, so you will probably have all sorts of interesting ideas about what to share and how.

You might also see gaps, things which feel like they are missing that we haven't covered – so you might have to create your own tasks or bits of performance to join the dots.

BUT! Don't forget to trust the process; if you've had a great time making, then the material will be great and you can trust that it is interesting.

You might have to refine and polish and rehearse it, to make sure everyone is really confident with what they're doing and how they're doing it. But remember you, and your stories, are enough!

THE PERFORMANCE . . .

We're excited about the idea of lots of different groups doing this, and how they will have the same starting points but take it in really different directions.

We would love every performance to include these things:

1. A beginning with the whole company on stage, where the prologue is delivered.

2. A dance moment at some point, created using the thanks for the dancing session.

3. The middle-logue somewhere in the middle.

4. At least three stories which are told, which are taken directly from the lives of company members onstage. Perhaps one could be the letter, one could be the story

about the inspiring figure, one could be the story about a song.

5.   A moment where the audience are asked to do a task.

6.   The epilogue at the end.

NOTE: you will find the text for the prologue, middle-logue and epilogue a bit later on!

It might feel quite different to what a 'normal' play feels like – that's all good! Maybe it might feel like a gig, or a fashion show, or an art exhibition? That's all great!

You're aiming for about 30 minutes. You want it to be long enough that you can include lots of different ideas, but not so long it starts to feel like too big a mountain to climb.

6. A PATH TO PERFORMANCE

NOW, some of you might think – how on earth do we begin to shape all this into a show?

So we've got a pathway for you to follow here if it is helpful!

You don't have to do this! Or you might start with this, and then think – nah we have better ideas.

Think about what moments might be interesting or surprising to be performed next to each other. A really tender moment, followed by something big and bold and silly. A moment where you talk about something big and epic like the future of the world followed by a moment you talk about something small and intimate like your favourite pair of socks . . .

SO! If you want it. A potential running order for the show.

THANKS FOR NOTHING

1. The prologue – use the text provided below, performed in a way that you think will resonate with the audience.

2. Dance break one: A moment of dance with the full company, with a song that was chosen by the group, which came out of the thank you for the music session. Perhaps it is just an extract before we see it in full later?

3. Lists of thanks and no thanks. People share, in quick fire, the things they are thankful and not thankful for. Big things, small things. Fun, silly, playful.

4. Thank you for writing – one person reads the letter they wrote.

5. Introduce the audience to the thank you monster. Perhaps the monster is quite shy and takes a bit of coaxing, but then gets confident and comes out to greet the audience and thank them for coming.

6. Thank you for trying – do some impossible tasks – LIVE! Perhaps these are tasks the company has never seen, but they pick them out of a hat and have to attempt to do them live in front of the audience. Maybe one cast member has 30 seconds to high five everyone in the audience. Maybe the whole cast has to improvise a song together straight away.

7. Moment where we get the audience to do a task to explore thankfulness.

8. Middle-logue, like the prologue, is performed in the way you think will be clear and compelling for the audience.

9. Ocean of gratitude – flood the whole space with this ocean you created.

10. Catwalk moment. We know what the audience *really* want, glamorous costumes, fancy sets; well, then, here we go. Show them what you've made!

11. Dance break two: The music starts, but perhaps nobody dances, they just listen, and then we hear the story why that song is important to somebody.

12. Thanks for the world you've given us! Speeches about the mess that young people have been given – angry!

13. Thanks for the future. We are taken through the things the young people have packed for the future.

14. Another letter from someone.

15. Dance routine. We hear that same song for the third time and the company moves in their own way that they choreographed together.

16. Epilogue.

7. THINGS YOU'LL NEED

THE PROLOGUE

> *Everyone is on stage, the whole company, performers, writers, designers. It's up to the company how this prologue is performed. By one person? By different people? Some parts spoken together?*
>
> *MAYBE it is spoken in almost total darkness and the lights come up over the course of the speech. Or the other way round.*

Hello! And welcome to the show!
The play is called *Thanks for Nothing*!
It is set here, in this room, right now.
The characters are us.
The stories are all ours.
And the audience that will help us make tonight what it is
is you!

We started making this play on [insert day]
We didn't get given a script or a plot or a dramatic arc. We didn't get given costumes or props or songs to sing.
We didn't get lots of words from some important playwright.
We had ourselves.
We were given a bunch of tasks, challenges and games.
We thought . . .
Thanks for nothing!

But we used those tasks and games to create what you will see tonight.

We thought about what we are grateful for. What we are not grateful for. And what gratitude looks, sounds and feels like.

And we will share something of what we found out with you, right now.

Brace yourselves cos we're gonna wade on in there right now. Leave the shore behind and let the waves carry us out to sea.

So. let's go!

THE MIDDLE-LOGUE

It's about the middle of the show now. Sort of, roughly.

This bit gets said at every performance of this show, whoever does it, wherever they do it. Like the prologue you heard at the beginning and the epilogue you will hear at the end.

This is the middle-logue; not sure that's the right word but never mind.

Everything else is from us; it's what we talked about, it's what we care about, it's what we wanted to share.

The PappyShow found it useful to think of this whole thing like a deep sea dive.

Maybe that'll be helpful for you?

You've got your scuba gear on and we're just diving down.

Deeper, and deeper and deeper.

To see what we find.

What strange and surprising creatures and features exist in the vastness below the surface?

It's all one ocean, but it's an infinity of life.

There are a lot of very different things in it. And they are always moving.

We won't see it all, not right now.

But we're lucky, I think, to get to swim in these waters together. Even for a while.

Anyway, Let's get back to the show.

THE EPILOGUE

So that was it.

That was *Thanks for Nothing*.

Well that was this version of *Thanks for Nothing*, this very specific version which was what it was because we were all here, in this exact moment, us as the company and you as audience, and we all gave exactly what we gave.

We are glad you came. It was good to have you here. Thanks for listening. Thanks for taking the time.

It's a funny thing after you've done a show, there can be a funny feeling of emptiness. Or giddiness. The adrenaline sometimes stays racing in your body long after the performance. So thank you in advance for being patient with us if we are in a funny mood later.

Thank you for wading out in the ocean with us. For diving deep. For noticing the little glowing dots of life in the dark waters, the pearlescent coral, the snaking creatures with fangs lurking on the sea bed, the tentacled beasts curled amongst the rocks. The deep sea trench filled with mysterious life which we will maybe never quite know or understand.

That ocean is always there to explore. The ocean of gratitude. You can go back and visit anytime.

But we're going to leave you now.

So thank you. And GOOD NIGHT!

BUT WAIT!

It's not over yet.

There is one more session left . . .

THANKS FOR THE MEMORIES

Now, your show was amazing, of course, and rightly you're all feeling proud and delighted and basking in the glow of it. But what next? It's time to draw things to a close just for yourselves.

Here are some ideas for this session:

In small groups create a photo album of the process with your bodies. Snapshots of the things that really stuck with you on this journey. Find a way to link these snapshots together with movement, music, text, whatever works for you.

Take a moment to write on a piece of paper what you are thankful for from this process. It might just be a few words. It might be something big and broad, it might be one specific moment. Then put them all in a box and lock it away and don't open it for a year. Or ten years.

In small groups create a piece that asks: where are you all in twenty years time? Or fifty years? Are you all connected? What is this group doing? It does not have to be literal. It might be a drawing, it might be a piece of dancing. Share the pieces with each other.

Write to us! We, The PappyShow, would LOVE to hear from you. Write us a letter, one letter, from the whole group. Tell us what this process has been like for you. What have you learned that might be interesting for us to know? What do you want to tell us? Send us it as an email so that it's easy to get to us from wherever you are:

admin@thepappyshow.co.uk

Photo credit: Dina Tsesarsky

Finally, in a big circle, do a check-out for the whole process. Give this TIME. Perhaps the three questions everyone answers are:

1. What will you take from this process?

2. What are you still trying to understand about gratitude?

3. What would you like to say to the rest of the group?

AND THAT'S IT!
Thanks for EVERYTHING
The PappyShow

Photo credit: Heather Carpenter

Revolting
by Bryony Kimmings

Contents

Part 1 – Inspiration

Firstly, hello. Thanks for choosing *Revolting*.

This is a little bit from me, the writer Bryony Kimmings, about what this is. Picking up this book is not like opening a script and finding characters, stage directions and act breaks.

I am an expert in making shows that move, surprise, motivate and change the audiences who watch them. But they are not fictional, they are all based on events in my own life. I make autobiographical, experimental devised theatre. This book is to show you how to do this yourself.

It may be a bit different to how you've worked in theatre before, if you have at all. Or it may serve as an update or fresh perspective to those of you who are a dab hand at devising. But don't worry, whatever your level, novice to expert, I have broken my process down into manageable chunks with examples and exercises.

So, buckle up. Let's do this.

Love Bryony x

What the hell is this?

THIS IS A SELF-GENERATED PLAY.

- I am going to give you a map for devising your own show.

- If you follow the instructions, you will create something wholly unique and inspiring . . . because it comes from your individual minds.

- The beauty is nothing can ever be wrong. I give you the outlines, you get the fun bit of colouring it all in!

THIS IS A SELF-GENERATED PLAY.

- I am going to tell you some of my show-making secrets.

- This is about YOU . . . all my shows are based in reality; it is never fictional people having fictional conversations about fictional things in fictional places.

- It can be a solo, duo or made by a group.

- It can be made in approximately ten sessions

THIS IS A SELF-GENERATED *PLAY* . . . SO LET'S PLAY!

FIRST, I suggest reading this whole instruction manual through together before you start. That way you won't be worrying about what is ahead. Up to you though.

Revolting

Your show is going to be called *Revolting*. I made that decision for you. This word is nice because it means two things . . .

Something disgusting: 'Urgh that is revolting'

AND

Something being reacted against:
'the peasants are revolting'

I liked the multi-layered meaning of the statement:

'This is revolting so we are revolting'

I always try to make shows that change the world. Yours is a show about being sick with elements of the current system and trying to change it; about being disgusted and inspired to act; about dreaming big and not caring about the things that will try and stop you . . . whatever your interpretation of 'revolting' this is a show about CHANGE.

Psssst, listen – a quick word . . . The dictionary definition of revolting uses the word 'violent action'. I do not believe that the word 'violent' must naturally mean physically hurting. It can also be symbolic violence (not working, not being physical, not speaking) or intellectual violence (outsmarting, changing public consciousness to hurt a system). I am not condoning physical violence or illegal activity. That would be wrong of me. Thanks. Bye xx

---

Finding your tribe

You may be placed in groups or select your own. You may know each other well or not at all. Or you may be working alone. The most important thing in any collaborative team is to know one another. Really well. So, let's start by establishing who you are as individuals.

Exercise 1 – Quick artistic statement

I want you to write down the following things individually . . .

* The three words that your best friend would use to describe you (quiet, thoughtful and sleeps anywhere or loud, rude and forever kind)

* The three subjects you are always blathering on about (boys, neurodiversity and *EastEnders*)

* The three things you like the look of most (1930s skyscrapers, shiny pebbles and empty restaurants)

* The three things you would love to hear someone say when they encountered something you made (wow she's funny, I feel moved, I want to dance)

When you have done that . . . fit it into this format:

Quick Artist Statement

Bryony Kimmings is ☐ , ☐ and ☐

She makes work about ☐ , ☐ and ☐

It feels like ☐ , ☐ and ☐

Audience's leave saying ☐ , ☐ and ☐

Voila!

Share these as a group. Get to know things about one another you didn't know. Notice where you are similar and different.

Now do you think you can create a company name and come up with a similar statement for the company? What does it look like when these people come to together?

Rules of the group

You are about to go on a journey into the unknown together. To get revolting.

Here are some rules . . .

1. Be respectful: this often means to think before speaking

2. Speak your truth: tell the *truth* about how things in the world make you feel

3. Be kind to one another: listen and try to understand even if you don't agree

4. Be a sponge: open your mind to the possibility that you don't know anything about anything. Inquisitiveness is your best friend when creating.

5.   Watch out for revelation: it lies around every corner and will change your course. Try to strike the right balance between focus and freedom; the show will show you the way. None of you should say no immediately. It shuts down ideas.

Exercise 2 – Guardian and scribe

You need to assign two people . . . this doesn't give those people any extra status in the group; the tasks just suit their personality type or who has time.

A guardian of this text – the person who knows this book inside out and can refer back to it as well as plan schedules using it. If you are stuck, I guarantee the answers lie in these pages, so it's good if someone knows it extra well. Who is this person?

A scribe – as you are generating this play, it needs to be written down as you go along, so it isn't forgotten. Pick a person/s to ensure this happens. This shouldn't mean that person/s can't participate fully. Who is this in your group?

Your room

You are now officially a company with your assigned guardian and scribe. You are going to be working closely together in a stressful, time-sensitive way. This means you need to take care of one another in the room you create in so you can make your best work. I would suggest this as a session structure.

- Arrive in the space, change out of your clothes and into comfy show-making stuff.

- Bring snacks, comforters, fidget toys, chocolate, paper and pens, and water.

- Do a warm-up all together and have fun with it; this is meant to be enjoyable. So, you are stretched and warm and in the mood.

- Have a check-in. Not too long or in-depth. Perhaps, how I am feeling about myself today, how I am feeling about the world today and what is inspiring me for this show today?

- Create a system where people can bow out, ask for a break, ask for apologies and seek help without being shamed.

- Take regular breaks and work through a handful of exercises in a session. Not the whole damn thing. Divide my exercises by the number of sessions you have and you have a rough schedule.

- Use the walls, spread ideas out all over the place, make visual reminders, let the room hold the collective brain of the company. Even if you have to take it down and put it up again each session, it's important it feels like YOUR space and it evolves with your show.

- When things start getting practical instead of talky, commit to always having a sharing at the end of a session. It may feel like you have nothing but getting anything up on its feet is key to how I create work. (See later pages.)

- Use my feedback techniques to make decisions to avoid conflict. (See later pages.)

- Do a check-out about feelings. Then speak to the Guardian about anything to bring or homework to do for the next session.

- The scribe can then write up anything that is needed so your working document comes in the next session updated (this person should get the most chocolate!)

Activism, Politics and Economy . . . yuck!

Ok, so before we start, we need a few pages of info about some gross things. If we are to find something *revolting* and start *revolting,* we have to get our hands dirty.

Immediately the title of this section would have put me off at your age. I definitely didn't know what these words exactly meant and I would have told myself it was because I was thick. So, I am translating them just in case. So, we are all on the same page.

An activist: a person who acts to bring about political or social change.

Politics: The activities associated with the *governance* of a country/area (making and upholding the law).

Economy: The distribution, control and creation of wealth and resources (money and stuff).

We have decided that *Revolting* is about CHANGE. This means you are automatically activists: people seeking change.

You can be interested in social change: friendships, family, school, etc.; or internal change: your self-esteem, your mental health, etc. Or you can be interested in global change . . . laws, policy, decisions . . . BUT know that however you spin it, all these areas are political and will inevitably somehow concern money too. Activism. Politics. Economy.

Left vs Right

Exercise 3 – Left wing vs right wing

Take a look at this diagram (also attached as a resource).

Often you will hear people discussing left-wing or right-wing politics. It took me a long time to truly get this.

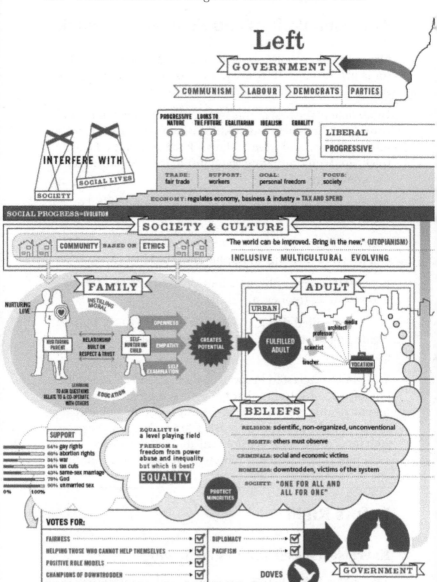

CREATIVE CREDIT
David McCandless & Stefanie Posavec // v1.2 // Dec 2010
InformationIsBeautiful.net / ItsBeenReal.co.uk

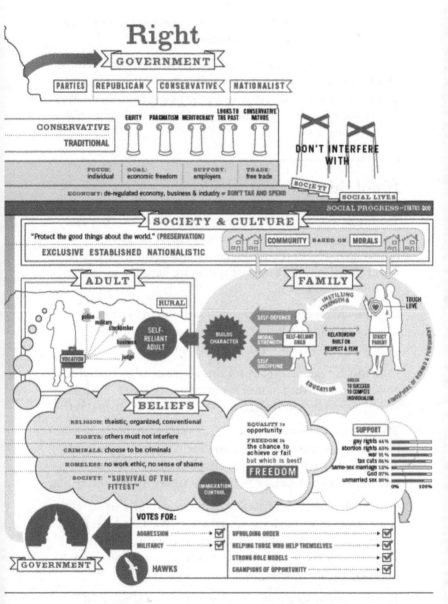

Right

GOVERNMENT

| PARTIES | REPUBLICAN | CONSERVATIVE | NATIONALIST |

CONSERVATIVE
TRADITIONAL

EQUITY · PRAGMATISM · MERITOCRACY · LOOKS TO THE PAST · CONSERVATIVE NATURE

DON'T INTERFERE WITH

FOCUS: individual · GOAL: economic freedom · SUPPORT: employers · TRADE: free trade

SOCIETY

SOCIAL LIVES

ECONOMY: de-regulated economy, business & industry = DON'T TAX AND SPEND

SOCIAL PROGRESS=STATUS QUO

SOCIETY & CULTURE

"Protect the good things about the world." (PRESERVATION)

EXCLUSIVE ESTABLISHED NATIONALISTIC

COMMUNITY BASED ON MORALS

ADULT

RURAL

police, military, stockbroker, business, judge

VOCATION

SELF-RELIANT ADULT

BUILDS CHARACTER

SELF-DEFENCE

MORAL STRENGTH

SELF DISCIPLINE

SELF-RELIANT CHILD

FAMILY

INSTILLING STRENGTH &

TOUGH LOVE

RELATIONSHIP BUILT ON RESPECT & FEAR

STRICT PARENT

EDUCATION SKILLS TO SUCCEED TO COMPETE INDIVIDUALISM

ATMOSPHERE OF REWARD & PUNISHMENT

BELIEFS

RELIGION: theistic, organized, conventional

RIGHTS: others must not interfere

CRIMINALS: choose to be criminals

HOMELESS: no work ethic, no sense of shame

SOCIETY: "SURVIVAL OF THE FITTEST"

EQUALITY is opportunity

FREEDOM is the chance to achieve or fail but which is best?

FREEDOM

IMMIGRATION CONTROL

SUPPORT

gay rights 44%
abortion rights 43%
war 81%
tax cuts 84%
same-sex marriage 13%
God 87%
unmarried sex 80%

0%   100%

VOTES FOR:

AGGRESSION	☑	UPHOLDING ORDER	☑
MILITANCY	☑	HELPING THOSE WHO HELP THEMSELVES	☑
		STRONG ROLE MODELS	☑
HAWKS		CHAMPIONS OF OPPORTUNITY	☑

GOVERNMENT

INEVITABLE CAPITALIST AGENDA

from the new infographic book of visual exploria

The Visual Miscellaneum

This is the best I've ever seen the difference in opinion about how our country can be run explained.

Can you study the diagram and discuss where your personal beliefs sit? Don't argue or criticise, just hear where you are all coming from. It's healthy to know these similarities and differences if you are working togevs! It also may change as you go along too!

If not this . . . then what?

This show is about looking at our problems as a society and attempting to do our bit to change them. Personally, I believe that a lot of the problems we face in the Western world stem from the financial system we have chosen to operate in: capitalism.

Capitalism: an economic and political system in which a country's trade and industry are controlled by private owners for profit, rather than by the state.

Individuals making money for themselves, rather than the government making money for everyone to share. We live within a capitalist society. In the UK we have a free market.

The idea of 'Free-market capitalism' is that anyone is free to bring stuff to market. This creates the illusion of equality. If anyone can make money, then anyone can have worth in society. If you don't make money this is your own fault.

Self-worth in the eye of society in the twenty-first century comes from how much money we can make, how high we can rise in the ranks of both earning and status/popularity, and how quickly we can do this. Success is measured in numbers (£, likes, views).

If our worth in society comes from a numerical value NOT a human value (like kindness or empathy or your happiness level) then you could say we live in a system where money is the most important thing. It trumps feelings.

Exercise 4 – Are you happy with that?

Are you happy with that? Talk through your own experience of capitalism, how it affects your life, how you feel about it.

Now, the free market has a flaw. It could only be truly perfect if every single person was born equal and was given equal opportunity, funds and access to education to enter the market. It would also mean that everyone was born with supportive, loving people around them. When we look at our world, we know this isn't true.

Many of the reasons people feel unhappy with a capitalist society is that the free market is not free at all. Only the rich can be involved whilst everyone else gets less and less.

Add to this the fact that modern capitalism is centred around generating a feeling of anxiety. It has been figured out that if the majority of people feel anxious about their worth they will spend more money, work harder to fit in.

So, we have an unequal society pretending to be equal, that wants us to feel anxious so we consume more and make the rich richer. That sounds pretty sucky for most of the population. You may have heard people talk about the 1 per cent. These are the people who benefit most from capitalism.

Exercise 5 – If not this . . . then what?

I want you guys to truly to discuss the statement:

'If not this . . . then what?'

But I would invite you to do this with someone who is an expert.

Can you find someone to talk to you about alternatives to the current system . . . a politics teacher at school, for example? Or perhaps one of these guys:

https://youthpolitics.org.uk/

It really is fascinating! It's been long debated about how the world should be run.

This work will give you a solid understanding to work from.

Rage list

Ok, now it is time to find the RAGE!

All my work starts with a feeling of injustice; a dark deep feeling in my stomach that believes humans deserve and can do better. Currently I am personally angry about:

1. Our mainstream apathy towards climate change

2. The slump in my self-esteem I feel when I engage with social media too much

3. Some parts of my family and their political beliefs

4. The way in which the world isn't designed for the neurodivergent (I am ADHD and my son is autistic)

5. The way in which homeless people are seen and treated in the UK

6. Trans exclusionary radical feminists (TERFS) and their growing platform

7. The lack of fair healthcare for black women when pregnant and or new mothers.

Exercise 6 – Rage list

I want you to think about your lives and write down (individually) what you are angry with . . . then get together and share these lists.

Note where you overlap, note which ones are infectious once discussed.

One of these is going to inspire your show . . . so hold onto the ones you can all agree on.

Make a group rage list.

Hope list

It is very important for me to say this next bit, as someone who has felt wholly depressed, worried and powerless in the world: you are not going to solve the world's problems during this time. I am not asking you to.

Please do not send yourselves into a deep spiral of hating the world and everyone living in it. That of course has its place; the world is sometimes unbearably cruel. But the world will change through a series of small actions by millions of small people. You are being asked to find your part in this.

When I feel overwhelmed with my rage list, I write a hope list. This is my current one:

Did you know trees have their own version of medicine under the ground and up in their canopy? They share nutrients, water and messages about disease with one another. They care about one another's survival knowing they all benefit from being next to one another. Be like a tree.

MacKenzie Scott has donated over $4 billion to charity since 2019 after receiving her divorce settlement from Jeff Bezos (the founder of Amazon and the richest man in the world). She has vowed to donate nearly all of her settlement to those in need. She doesn't believe any human needs more money than they can spend in a lifetime. Be a Scott, not a Bezos.

When polled in 2020 the UK population stated that the most important thing in their lives was love. Not money. Love.

When babies are born, they are guided to their mother's breast by a dark line that forms on the stomach of their mother. The mother's areola (bit around the nipple) also darkens so the baby (who only sees in black and white) can follow the line and then find food. Imagine the mother's body like a landing strip for a plane, like a natural map. We know how to live in the balance of nature inherently, we are animal.

The horrific murder of George Floyd in 2020 (and countless other black people before and since) reignited the Black Lives Matter movement to a scale never seen before. There were protests in over 6000 towns and cities across the world during a pandemic! It is estimated that 10 per cent of the entire American population were moved to the streets. People power works.

Exercise 7 – Hope list

If you think it would be helpful,

create your own hope list to look at!

Part 2 – Preparation

Let's start making your version of *Revolting*.

The Blitz and Trick System

I make my work following a rigorous system. I teach this system. I write about this system. I use it; and it works. It isn't designed for you to make work like **me**, it is about how to give you the tools and confidence to make work like **you**.

It gives you a tool kit and a structure to sessions that eliminate the creator's biggest fear:

Empty page. Empty stage.

My mum always says, 'You can't eat an elephant whole'. For years I just thought this was a weird thing to say . . . who eats elephants?! In later life I realised what she meant. Breaking a large task down into bitesize chunks stops you from feeling overwhelmed by the enormity of the whole.

I am ADHD and have spent a lot of my creative life before diagnosis trying to figure out ways to trick myself into creating without my natural doubt and negative internal monologue kicking in. My distractions and my limited concentration span have meant I have created a system full of short sharp bursts of activity. That's why it's called Blitz and Trick.

I have based my entire creative practice around a very important truth about theatre. And it's a secret not everyone knows . . . The only thing that matters in the theatre is the audience. You are simply providing them with the mirror to see themselves. At every turn of telling a story I have them at the front of my mind. Your job is to entertain, move and inspire them. You are a master of emotional manipulation.

So, you are angry about something, you are going to tell the audience why and then you are going to show them you tried to change it in the hope that they, at the end of the show, feel inspired to do so too. We are going to break the elephant down in this section.

Let's try it

Put a hidden camera in my studio at the beginning of any creation and the main thing you would watch would be me alternating between dancing like a maniac and writing like a maniac. Over and over before I took a nap or had a coffee and then I would do it again. High octane, short time span.

I like allowing myself no time to agonise and labour over decisions or editing in the early days.

A decision about anything in this life will very much show itself as wrong if it's wrong. If you do not take a decision you stay in the same place. You can go home and come back and be just as stuck the next day. Indecision is the kryptonite of art.

Blitz and Trick: The repetitive act of dancing like crazy for a minute and then doing a short writing exercise from the pumped-up part of your brain that doesn't even know it's being creative because of said dancing!

Exercise 8 – Questions

Grab your notebooks and a pen. Find a comfy space for yourself in the room. Place your book down. One of you take control of the book and the sound system (it would be so awesome if this wasn't a person in the group so y'all can participate) and be in charge of playing music for a minute then switching the tunes off and calling out the exercise and timing another minute before blasting off the tunes again. Everyone else do as this person says . . . it's a race against time and if you don't finish, never mind, up you get and start again. Think of it like art musical bumps. This is all about questions you have about the world and how it works. Things that consume your life and piss you off. You are working individually. Let's go . . .

- Dance

- Write five questions you have about the big wide world (politics, systems, injustice)

- Dance

- Write five questions that consume your everyday life (family, friends, feelings)

- Dance

- Write five questions that you wish you could ask someone but can't or don't dare

- Dance

- Write five questions that come from a very angry and bitter place

- Dance

- Write five you would like to ask on someone else's behalf

- Dance

- Write five questions that everyone is silently shouting in the streets.

Once you've finished this sit and share all your questions. Talk and laugh and rage about the things that inspire and ignite your fire. This is where activism begins. A fire. Can you find any questions that you all agree you want to know the answer to? Where do all of you unite?

That is where your revolt is going to happen.
In your collective fire.

Exercise 9 – Questions, questions

Together please pick three questions (from the above exercise or newly generated from the discussion you have had about collective fire) that all of you find inspiring. Everyone needs to write those three questions in their notebooks. Let's Blitz and Trick again. One minute dancing/one minute writing.

- Dance

- Pick a question from your selected three and write every OTHER question that comes out of it

- Dance

- Pick another question and do the same

- Dance

- And now do the same for the last question.

What we are seeing here is which one has the best 'legs'. It's a term I use a lot. Some subjects are interesting but I couldn't spend years of my life deep within them; there isn't enough interesting angles or material or I would tip my sanity over the edge. Which one of these questions has legs . . . which one interests and fires you up the most? Sit and read and consider this alone first, reading back your blitzed notes . . . then come together and discuss how you feel.

Now collectively choose which one you like best. This is what you find revolting as a group. This is your Topic Question. The question the show explores. It's as easy as that.

For the purposes of being able to give examples from this moment on I will use this one:

Why does any real engagement with climate change prevention (for us as individuals) feel too overwhelming, too impossible and too late?

Exercise 10 – Brain Dump

Whack your question into the centre of a massive roll of paper (big enough for you to all write on at once). Have a big dance all together to share the collective joy at being united over something. Then grab your books and whack all your questions that came from this question onto the Brain Dump . . . talking with each other, taking away duplicates, etc. Then have some fun putting other things onto the paper. Here are some suggestions. All stemming from your Topic Question in the centre.

- Films it makes you think of

- Images that feel relevant

- Articles to read

- Books to read

- Objects, set, costume that feel relevant.

- Sayings or phrases

- Music it makes you think of

No pressure, no quality control or curbing of ANYTHING; this Brain Dump is simply a place to dump ideas. Some of this stuff will make it into the show, some won't. But this paper is your collective brain, so you want to fill it up and talk about it all. Later you will narrow it down.

Understanding Story

To create a show first we must understand how a story works. This is because you are going to be telling one onstage. But also because in the following sections you are going to go out into the world and make a story happen (so you can tell it to us). So, this collection of exercises delves deep into understanding narrative (a posh way of saying story).

In the West we are taught how to tell a story from a very young age. Even the simplest books have the same narrative structure (story shape) as the most complex stories told by our greatest writers.

Understanding the world through stories is so innate that not only do we do it automatically when we read or watch a movie. We also tell our life stories in this way when we speak to one another. We also search for these narratives in abstract things like dance and paintings.

The idea of telling a story has always been a scary thing for me. I did not study playwriting, English or theatre. I have always felt therefore that there must be a secret I didn't know about, or indeed a heap of theory and understanding that meant I wasn't allowed to write stories. But in fact stories are very simple. I found knowing this incredibly empowering.

A story is simply this:

- We meet a person and that person is one way (we could call this a flaw)

- Something happens to them which challenges them or their lives

- They go through a period of trying to solve this problem or surmount the obstacle they are facing (this is called the quest)

- They solve the problem over a series of moments and they are changed because of the things they encounter (this usually neatly means the character becomes the opposite of their original flaw).

A story is essentially a character doing something that changes them or how they see the world. You do not want to watch a character start a certain way, go through a series of amazing and exciting events and feel nothing and not change as a person. Firstly, that is not humanly possible.

Secondly, that is very boring. We want to see what humans are made of.

It's all about change.

I have written a story down following the above instructions as an example:

A man is scared of other humans (flaw), so he lives alone with his dog and rarely leaves the house. He doesn't trust the world and he doesn't trust people.

His beloved dog goes missing. He thinks it has been stolen (something happens).

He believes that whoever stole his dog is travelling by car as unfamiliar tyre tracks are visible at the scene. So, he sets off across America to find his beloved dog finding clues along the way (the quest: to get his dog back).

Along the way he meets people and encounters situations as he searches, and each one changes him slightly. He meets a man who has lost everything in a war but yet he manages to get out of bed every day and live in hope he will find new things to love. He meets a family living with no food on their table but huge love and respect for one another and it makes them kings. He encounters a lady surrounded by people but incredibly alone. He watches her reveal her true self and lose many fake people but find an incredible loyal few who love her more.

When he finds his dog, he realises that the person who stole it is more scared of humans than he is. He decides that he no longer needs the dog and that he is ready to live in the world without fear. So, he lets the thief keep the dog but tells him the story of his journey to inspire him to go out into the world like he did instead of being scared.

He is changed (he is now the opposite of his flaw, he becomes brave).

1. Who's story is it?

2. What does the character need?
(What is theur flaw? What do they need to learn)

3. What is the inciting incident?

4.What does the character want?

5. What obstacles are in the character's way?

6. What's at stake?

7. Why should we care?

8. What do they learn?

9. How and why?

10. How does it end?

Copyright: John Yorke

Exercise 11 – Movies

Can you choose a movie you have all seen and write it down like I have just done with my example?

I often use *The Lion King* (which is actually the story of *Hamlet*!).

Even stories that are told out of order when written logically in terms of events will follow this formula (like the film *Memento* for example).

Do this together and chat it out.

Exercise 12 – Choose your own adventure

Now try and write your own version of a story like I did in the example. Read them to one another and discuss.

Pssst, when I am writing I find this graphic from John Yorke (on the previous page) very helpful. If you can answer all ten questions you can write a story. If you get stuck it is usually because there is an answer missing. So, it's a nice way to check off the parts you need before you start.

What story shall we tell in *Revolting*?

You are going to tell the story of how you (as a group, duo or a solo person) changed from revolted (disgusted) to revolting (trying to enact change). From passive to active. From powerless to powerful.

Inspired by your Topic Question, you are going to go out and do something in the real world that changes you all in some way. And then you are going to tell us the story of what happened; probably in great costumes and with loads of glitter or plate smashing (in my mind!)

NOTE: me telling you what your story is about will immediately start your brain firing off in all directions. So, remember my mum's elephant. You do not know this story yet as you haven't done anything. So don't start worrying. I will take you through how to do this all step by step. Promise.

Who were we before?

Exercise 13 – Flaws

It would be a really good idea to spend a moment just jotting yourself down as a character.

Hi, I'm Bryony, I am an ADHD, 40-year-old woman and trauma survivor with trust issues, a lot of self-loathing and a little problem with confidence. But I am also a very hopeful person, who likes to see the best in people and give my time and love generously. I love laughing. I'd do anything for my family. I have a big chip on my shoulder about class.

Who are you, guys? It might feel weird, but later we will need these descriptions to find the flaw we need in each of you to tell the story.

Exercise 14 – Becoming an expert

Before your next session I think it would be great to do some light reading, watching and researching in your chosen area of focus.

If your question concerns trans rights perhaps divvy up some research reading so ya'll can come to the next session with some extra knowledge.

It might also be good to start a group where you share info together outside of session. I would say WhatsApp, but I know that makes me old! Gaaaaaaaa!

Look at your Brain Dump and share this work out.

Social experiments

I am a social experimentalist. Probably not a word that you've heard many others say about themselves. In short as a job, I go out into the world and do something extraordinary to try and change it. I identify a problem, I do something out in the field to fix it, then I make a show about it.

You are going to become social experimentalists to make this show. Yup. Exciting I know!

A bit about my work . . .

Very early in my career I decided that theatre was not an egalitarian thing like say telly or film. It was reserved for the elite, people with money, and had a certain cultural currency. It became important to me to change that. I grew up on a council estate and didn't see theatre until I was sixteen. I found I liked the shows that had something to say about real life. Live performance is unique, powerful and should be for EVERYONE. It is humans living and breathing together in a room, more immediate and active than watching a film or reading a book. I wanted to reach people both in the theatre seats, but also out in the real world, and even through someone reading about my outlandish experiment in the paper. To try and make it more egalitarian and give more people access. So, I decided to make shows about my life.

Previous social experiments I have done:

In 2014 I became a pop star for a year; invented and managed by my nine-year-old niece. We tried to explode the tween marketing world from the inside out by creating an alternative.

In 2015 I asked my partner to quit his high-powered capitalist marketing job to tour around the world performing a show about his hidden and crippling depression to allow other men to talk about mental health.

In 2016 I turned a group of fifty lads from council estates into a feminist peace army for change.

In 2017 I collaborated with twenty cancer patients to make a musical about the realities of life with cancer.

In 2021 I made an opera with and about the lives of single mums. I wanted the world to see just how dramatic that small and hidden world really was.

Exercise 15 – Your social experiment

Together I want you to look at your Topic Question and I want you to come up with some ideas of how to change your feeling of powerlessness into something powerful, an act of revolution. What could you do in the real world to change yourselves, and thus a small part of the world? I would suggest Blitzing and Tricking for this exercise so you are being light and inquisitive. But first let me give you an example. For my question:

Why does any real engagement with climate change prevention (for us as individuals) feel too overwhelming, too impossible and too late?

Here are some ideas for social experiments:

- For three weeks we are going to live off grid as if the world as we know it has ended due to climate change and see how we survive

- We are going to work with the least likely climate activists in our lives (be it us or people we know) and change the way they live to fit the guidance provided by Greenpeace as to how to live in accordance with the planets' needs

- We are going to live off foraged foods for one month without breaking the law

- We are going to try and change a policy that frustrates us in our local community through lobbying, protest and people power

- We are going to sit in our cafeteria until the school agrees to change the food they provide to be low carbon emission

- We are going to create a place for people to go to understand what the world would look like if we don't do anything to change

- We are going to remove all toxic living (unethical brands, single-use plastics, foods from outside of the UK, not use fossil fuels) from our lives and see how we feel.

Blitz and Trick . . .

- Dance

- Write one social experiment idea down each for your Topic Question

- Dance

- And another

- Dance

- And another

Now sit together and share all of the ideas for social experiments.

Choose which one you like best, which one helps you change your revolting into revolting so to speak. Of course, it needs to be possible – you can't go to the moon, for example – but it should also feel outlandish, difficult and scary. You have to find a challenge that scares you and go full frontal into it to see what happens.

Write down your social experiment.

OMG you just made a brave decision; pat each other on the back!

For the purpose of the example I have chosen: We are going to sit in our cafeteria until the school agree to change the food, they provide to be low carbon emission.

Exercise 16 – The rules

This is your act of revolt. You are doing something outside of your norm to change a part of the world you don't like. And that thing you are doing is not what people normally do so it takes planning. Lean into outlandish, extraordinary, bold decisions as you write your rules down and plan your experiment. I always suggest Blitz and Trick just in between to keep the blood flowing and stop a huge static discussion meaning you start to get scared!

- Set yourself a time frame – this can be time based or action based. For two weeks we live like wolves or we do this until we get chucked out.

- Set yourself a tangible goal – in my example the change of the food to be low carbon emission. You are choosing something you can measure success by, a change you want to see. Even if you fail it's okay; some of the best stories are about what happens to people when they fail.

- Set your safety parameters and gather the things and people you need to support you

- Try to film as much of it as you can!

- Plan your time carefully, what will you do and when, who is doing what, etc

- Find a way to chart your successes and failures. Have something that means you can measure them

- Chart the changes in how you feel about your subject and yourself; this is very important. Use a video diary, journaling, recorded discussion

- Have regular meetings to chart where you are at and offer support to one another

- Let the people who need to know what you are doing know. They can make sure you are not doing anything harmful to others or yourself, or illegal.

Exercise 17 – Flaws 2

Before you go out and start doing stuff let's just do something that will be helpful later. Let's quickly go back to the text we wrote about ourselves in **Exercise 13 – Flaw**. Which part of you is the most accurate for how you feel right now?

For my example: I feel a bit triggered by the idea of having to do a sit-in protest; people will look at me, judge me, etc. My confidence feels low. Ok, this is good. My character flaw is: lack of confidence. So, as I chart the changes in me it is this flaw I am measuring against.

Now out you go and do it!

And don't come back to this book until you are done!

Dramatic Pause . . .

Part 3 – Creation

Hiya! How the hell was that?!

You will now have a shed load of information on what happened and documentation of it. Get out your old Brain Dump too and spread yourself out into your room again. Recap your room rules, reconnect with a nice warm-up game and get your heads in gear . . . Because you are going to start making your show now!

We are now going to make some key decisions in the coming pages about how to turn all of this stuff into a piece of theatre.

Exercise 18 – How do I feel?

Look back at **Exercise 17 – Flaws 2**.

How do you feel now? In comparison.

Is it the opposite?

Did you change?

How do you feel as a group?

Was there also a collective change: disempowered to empowered? Chat about it. Write stuff down.

Finding the story

Once you have done your experiment you will need to find the story. Remember earlier we talked about how stories work, how people are constantly looking for them. Organise what happened to you guys into a story.

Here are the parts again:

- We meet a person or group of people that are one way

- Something happens to them which challenges them or their lives

- They go through a period of trying to solve this problem or surmount the obstacle they are facing

- They solve the problem over a series of moments and they are changed because of the things they encounter

- The person or group is changed by what happened (they become their opposite).

In my example that might read like this:

- A group feel broke, fearful and paralysed to act against climate change. (Flaw)

- The group discover that one pizza in the school cafeteria has the carbon footprint of running a car for a whole year. (This starts the story; they've had enough)

- The group decide to sit in the cafeteria until the school changes how they run the place; it feels like something they can actually do . . . sitting. It costs nothing and it is symbolic

- The headteacher shows his true colours when he tries to have them ejected; we get scared at night when there is no one there; one of us gives up because their mum is cross; the dinner ladies are angry and want to kick the kids out

- Then one of the dinner ladies sits one evening with the group and charts how many air miles the food for one week has flown and she is shocked and sad; the local radio come and interview the group who use this airmiles info to inspire the whole community. In turn the whole school and some parents come and sit in the cafeteria in solidarity until the headteacher caves in and changes the whole system to lower the carbon footprint

- The group realise that every person can do small things to change the world; it is multiple tiny actions the world over that will change the planet's future. (They are the opposite of who they were in the beginning.)

Exercise 19 – Your story

Decide amongst yourselves how to write your story down. Please note it's OK to embellish and turn up the dial of emotion if you wish – this is theatre, darling! Write your story down.

This is the narrative of your show.

Exercise 20 – Story map

Please watch this video: https://www.youtube.com/ watch?v=oP3c1h8v2ZQ. It's an oldie but a goodie. Then please draw the shape of the story you have written onto a very big piece of paper like Kurt Vonnegut does in the video.

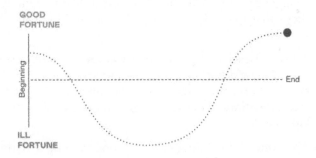

Now place each of the events of your story along that line. This is your Story Map; these events will be scenes. Please draw a box around each event, with enough space to write in other details. The first will probably be introducing who you were before and your flaw; the end will probably be who you were after, flaw changed. It will look a bit like this: a series of empty boxes with brief scene headings along the line of your Story Map.

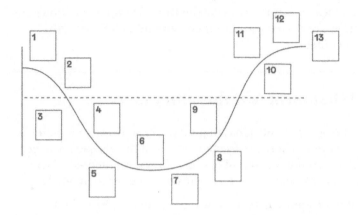

Each of these boxes are things we need to make. Don't worry, no elephant eating here, I am going to show you how in the following pages.

Adding information the audience also need to know

Exercise 21 – Facts and figures

I want you to go through your Brain Dump now with a fine-tooth comb along with all your notes from your social experiment . . . and stick subjects/information that the audience also need to know about your Topic Question into the boxes along the story map. Or even in between if you wish. This is because there will be some things you can't tell a story about until other information is given to the audience (for example, 'Here are ten facts about trans rights that you need to know before we continue').

It's a nice way to include all the stuff that inspired you in the first place by either hiding it within the story or even taking breaks for factual moments. The Story Map is a working document, I often scrap it and draw it all out again as I make and learn. It is time to take the Brain Dump down; don't bin it, but replace it with this more streamlined Story Map document.

What form will this story take?

The beauty of my job is that there are so many ways to tell a story live. There are so many forms of theatre/performance that I couldn't make all of those shows in a lifetime. That's exciting to me! Some forms fit stories better than others.

What I want you to do now is to really have fun with form. Let's find out the best way to tell this show.

Exercise 22 – Fun with form

This is a really funny Blitz and Trick. Someone man the music. Write the questions below on a big sheet of paper and stick them on the wall so everyone can see them. You are going to dance wildly and then take a couple of minutes to fill in the answers to these questions to create make believe versions of your show.

Questions:

What kind of show is this?

What is the main narrative driver?

What other mediums of communication do you use?

What is the visual theme?

What is the theme music?

What do the audience think this show is about and what is it really about?

THEATRE • DANCE • MIME • CABARET • FORUM • IMPROV • STAND UP
PUPPETRY • SEX SHOW • GAME SHOW • SHAKESPEARE • WALKING TOUR
INSTALLATION • OPERA • BALLET • PANTOMIME • QUIZ SHOW • SKETCH
• GREEK TRADEGY • ONE PERSON SHOW • COMMUNITY THEATRE • SITE
SPECIFIC • PERFORMANCE ART • FILM • MUSICAL • PLAY • DOCUMENTARY
THEATRE • LECTURE • DEVISED • BRECHTIAN • ONLINE • CHOOSE YOUR OWN
ADVENTURE • TWO-HANDER • THEATRE IN EDUCATION • THEATRE IN PRISONS
• KIDS SHOW • GIG THEATRE • WALKABOUT/PROMENADE • IMMERSIVE
CONCEPTUAL ALBUM • SITCOM • FEATURE FILM • CIRCUS • VARIETY
AGITROP • FLASH MOB • OPENING CEREMONY • SEANCE • DINNER PARTY
• 1-2-1 • CLOWN • YOUTUBE TUTORIAL • PLAYBACK • SIDESHOW • WEST END
SHOW • VAUDEVILLE • FUND RAISER • TELETHON • WORKSHOP • SOUND PIECE

Read this example out together beforehand to see what I mean; your versions should be a bit like this:

It's a circus show. We have a mic and take it in turns to tell the story directly to the audience from each of our perspectives. There are circus acts, songs, dancing and lecture style presentations with slides. It's a mash up! It's set in a cafeteria but the costumes and props are all circus themed (also carbon kept coming up in our brainstorms, so at some point carbon starts to pile up on the stage too, getting in the way of both the cafeteria and the circus). The music choices are all the greatest showman mixed with punk music. The audience think this is a show about the decline of the planet when really it is about small acts of solidarity and love in your community.

Blitz and Trick

• Dance

• Write one version following the questions on the wall.

• Dance

• Write another

• Dance

• Write another

You guys could do this 100 times and each would create a totally different show telling the same story. This is the fun of creativity. You don't want to look at that Story Map and tell the story like everyone else would, you want to tell in a way that is perfect to you and your experience and your tastes as a group.

Exercise 23 – Pitch to mates

You guys need to read all of these show descriptions to one another out loud. Have fun imagining each and every one of them. Then whittle them down to three. You might want to combine some, or tweak them . . . whatever you wish. You just need three descriptions written down.

When I am deciding what the show form will be. I pitch three options for the show to loads of mates. I give them a little info about my Topic Question and about my social experiment and then I pitch three ways I could tell the story. Could you gather together a group of people and pitch. Then get people to vote for which one they would pay money for a ticket for. Just one vote. Which one wins? That's the one to make.

Now you have your form . . . whoop!

Audience

Now we know the story we want to tell and how we plan to tell it. Next, I turn to the reason I am making this show THE AUDIENCE.

I pick three things I want my audience to leave with: an emotion, a decision and an action.

For my Climate Change example, I want my audience to leave my show . . .

- Devastated but hopeful
- Convinced people power could actually work
- Ready to join a group or cause

Exercise 24 – Audience aims

Can you do this for your show please.

Chose an emotion, a decision and an action.

Here is a trick. Imagine your audience before a show starts as this: A group of people who wish they had gone to get pizza instead of coming to the theatre sit down to watch your show, tired and a bit hungry.

When this same group leave you want them to feel what you decided for them.

"I don't want to be here; I wish I had gone for pizza" **changes to** *"I am devastated but hopeful, I am convinced people power could actually work and I am ready to join a group or cause."*

That huge shift, that massive change in them . . . that is now your job.

Each scene you create will take the audience on an incremental step towards that final state from that initial state.

Exercise 25 – Audience emotional journey

Into your boxes along your Story Map make a note of how you think your audience should feel in each scene. Note that they will pretty much feel like you guys do in the show, remember you are the mirror. There are over 34,000 emotions so lots to choose from and remember it can be complicated . . . the audience can feel torn, clashing emotions or from one emotion to another all in one scene so you don't need to be reductive. Take a look at this graphic for emotional inspiration.

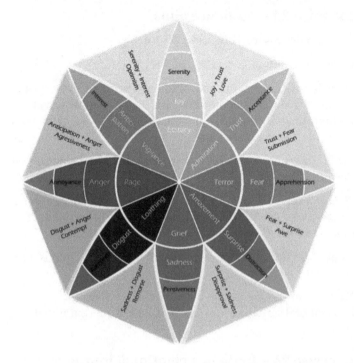

In each box add some info on the audience's emotional journey.

Then your job is simply to create the material to tell them this part of the story and make them feel how you want them to.

Ways to communicate

Exercise 26 – Communication tools

I like to keep a massive list of communication tools at my disposal in my studio so if I get stuck I just grab one randomly and make the scene using it. Here are some examples:

song, magic act, direct address (speaking directly to the audience), dance routine, poem, projection, storytelling, stand-up, opera, mime, puppetry, borrowed texts (essays, passages from books, facts), cooking, political speech, placards and slogans (written word), dialogue (scenes with people talking), real life act (smashing a watermelon), audience participation moment, interviews, lectures, building something, music videos, circus acts.

The list is endless. Can you generate some more? Now as a group can you choose a handful of options for each scene.

Scene one might be good as a song, but it could also be ace as a big section of projection, or it could be good as a circus act.

We are going to make a few versions of each scene to see which work best.

Exercise 27 – Stuff and nonsense

Before you come in next time, I want you to find things you want to use in this show.

Props, costumes, set pieces, projected videos, magic tricks, huge blackboards . . .

Next time you come into this space you will start making a show and it will be quick . . . so you want loads of fun things to play with!

Go back through all your notes and Brain Dump and see if anything leaps out you have forgotten.

You don't need to plan what you are doing with them . . . just have stuff in the space. Music too.

Making content

Let's make the show now. Bit by bit. I would very heavily suggest you create chronologically – it's easier.

You are going to make scenes by following a simple formula that I call 'Briefs'.

I got this phrase from working as a temp in an advertising firm after I finished school and thought it was an excellent way to tell stories and it could be applied to making theatre shows. In advertising the people who want to sell you things write very simple briefs as to how to capture your brain enough to make you buy said thing. 'I want people aged twenty-five to buy Coca-Cola; people of that age are currently interested in health. I want them to think Coca-Cola will make them healthy so they buy it.' Gross, right?

I am not trying to get people to buy things but I am wanting them to know and believe things and feel certain ways about them. So, I stole the idea and changed it a bit.

- I want to talk to you about...

- I want to use...

- I want to reveal...

- I want my audience to feel...

Here is an example brief for my climate show:

- I want to talk to you about . . . the moment that one of us left because their mum got angry

- I want to reveal . . . that despite what it looked like all of us wanted to go home in that moment

- I want to either use song, projection, dialogue or a circus act

- I want the audience to feel worried for us but excited to see what happens next.

What does that scene look like?

There is only one way to know: write it or get up and devise it. You know what info you need to get across, you know how you want the audience to feel and you have a few options to try out. This is the fun bit.

Exercise 28 – Write your briefs

Write briefs for each of your moments.

Then practically plan your next few sessions to have time to both make and share these moments.

You are literally going to build the show from the ground up: make/share/get feedback/make decision/move on.

Exercise 29 – Make in chunks

Chat about an idea conceptually and then give it a bash. Be playful. Make sure you document them. And start a little collection of the ones you think do their job best. Make sure the scribe also jots down or you video everything you make though; some material might be useful somewhere else if changed etc.

Example: Ok, so I really love the song 'Toxic' by Britney Spears. This scene is about how toxic this pizza is; it's covered in carbon footprint. So, we are going to dance to 'Toxic' dressed as air hostesses and cover a giant delicious pizza in carbon then try and eat it and feel sick.

Have fun, this is the best bit . . . you are finding your show! It will sort of just appear. Dance in between making to keep yourselves feeling engaged and take it in turns to plan sessions or have ideas, etc so you are all having a go. Don't over think it as a whole show. That is a mistake. That will ruin it. So just make each scene to brief. No elephant munching.

Sharing is caring

Once you have a few scenes to string together you will want to share them with some trusted people who can give you constructive feedback. (The creation process is vulnerable as you don't yet know all the answers or indeed sometimes what you want so you don't want a strong personality bulldozing in and tearing it all to bits; therefore choose your test audience carefully, people you love, who you trust, who will want to help!)

You chose a narrative driver a while back. Do you remember? **Exercise 22 – Fun with form**. In my shows it is usually direct address; in my example it is too. For me this is the easiest way to sew together the story beats by talking directly to the audience.

What I do is make a little chain of scenes with my narrative driver in between and share it with the audience. Sound simple? It is.

Here is a little chain of scenes for my example (I have marked whether it was content made from a brief which I have called 'scene' or the extra info we needed to pop in to make sure the next scene could happen, the 'narrative driver')

- Scene One: everyone comes onstage and introduces themselves in a fun and light way. They give a little detail of who they were before the story started (Hi, I'm Bilal, and before we did this, I couldn't have cared less about my carbon footprint). NARRATIVE DRIVER

- Scene Two: slapstick routine about the moment the group discovered the air miles of one pizza in the cafeteria using model planes and loads of fake carbon that covers them all in dust. SCENE

- Scene Three: Joe confesses to the audience he had no idea what carbon was then he uses a little slide projector to explain. NARRATIVE DRIVER followed by a SCENE

- Scene Four: lip-synch: one of the actors pretends to be the headteacher not giving a crap about the carbon footprint of his own cafe. SCENE

- Scene Five: all the characters dressed in army clothes tooling up for the cafeteria sit-in; it's funny as they are dressed for war but the plan they reveal (to occupy until the head changes his tune) is very peaceful. SCENE

- Scene Six: Emma confesses her heart wasn't in it to the audience because she was having trouble at home. NARRATIVE DRIVER

Feedback

Look at this graphic:

Audience Feedback

- What was it about?
- What did it reveal about the story or character?
- How did it make you feel?

This is what I ask my test audience at the end of a sharing.

Can you see how what you are asking your audience for in terms of feedback directly relates to the brief you made your work to? I aim to tell you X and I want you to feel Y. A sharing with feedback simply finishes the equation. Did you get X and did you feel Y?

I would normally do written feedback; I make sheets with questions and instructions. On my first sharing early in the making process I might pause after every single scene and let the audience feedback about that one part. I might even show multiple versions of the same scene if I can't choose which does the job best.

Later, as I test the material more, I become more interested in what the whole is starting to look and feel like so I'll show all of it in one (this is because I have already shown and got feedback for each part so I feel quite secure that it does what I intend). However complex the thing I am showing I always ask those same questions.

Exercise 30 – Time to get it up on its feet

I want you to organise a little sharing at the end of each making session for your own work using my feedback technique.

This will teach you far more about the material than discussing it in theory will ever do.

It's scary but you only truly understand a devised show when it is in front of an audience.

What to do with feedback

Exercise 31 – Reading feedback

Once you've shared gather up your feedback and read it together. You are checking whether the material does what you think it does to the audience. I often do this the next day. This is because I also learn a great deal about my material when I'm sharing. So, I'd like to let the dust settle on that first. If you read it straight away you can get a little wounded. Then as a group discuss your findings. But read this guidance first . . .

Personally, I'm looking for general consensus. Not every single person will view every story in the same way but you want to trust the common denominator. If everybody but one person is saying that a scene made them laugh when your intention was to make them cry, then you have to go with the general consensus and say that that scene was comedic as opposed to moving.

If you do not get the answers you want you can then discuss as a group why this might be, you can ask the audience why (especially if you know them well, so use that), you can rework the scene from the feedback and try again or indeed use the scene somewhere else where the emotion you were after is more fitting. You are building a show not talking about a show. Do it in the room.

In theory Revolting *is only ready when you have a show that completes your overall audience aims (how you get there remains fluid). You want an emotion, a decision and an action from your audience at the end. Your show is a beast that needs taming; every decision is based upon (not the taste of individual group members) audience experience. Sometimes I have scenes in my work I hate, but they do the job I need them to.*

Make a little plan of attack; we are going to try that again without smiling and with less hilarious music next time. We need an explanation about X before we show the Y scene. It's a technical process, so get technical and make decisions together with a theory of what that might do to a scene and why. Then go back into the room and change them and share them again.

Slowly the show will make itself. It is ready when the audience aim is complete.

Polishing

Once you have your whole show you want to set aside some time to polish it.

You want to find layering, call-backs, repetition, re-use of props and catchphrases so the individual scenes start to feel like a whole chain of events not just lots of tiny bits in a row. You also want what you have to feel really tight and seamless. The polish is the showbiz part. Lol.

So, when you are 'finished' spend a final session or two polishing. You might want to ask an outside eye (a trusted person to feedback critically and constructively) or dramaturg (someone who looks after the story and whether it makes sense) into the room and give them a specific instruction or two, or indeed perform it just as a group and watch out for these specific things yourself.

Exercise 32 – Look for links

Do a run of the show and make a list of things you or an outside eye/dramaturg are going to look for. This part is about showing the audience as oppose to telling. It's often where I cut down text.

Example

- Do we say the same thing twice? *Doubling up messages is normal but audiences hate it. It means they think you think they are stupid.*

- Is there a motif from the first few scenes that could be helpful later to remind the audience about something without having to repeat it? *When we do this movement, it will remind the audience of how naïve we were in the beginning; if we slow it down and make it hard to perform it will represent sorrow and failure.*

- Is there a catchphrase for this show and could it pop up in other places to help create meaning or remind us of previous scenes?

- Is there an object we could layer meaning on in an early scene that then represents something we can break later? *This apple represents hope in Scene One. Would it be good if it gets eaten late to show hope is gone? What about if at the end the final image is of lots of apples growing on a tree?*

- Are there places where the show lags, are there too many things in a row that feel the same tempo, emotion or style? *Are there things we can put in between to keep our and the audience's energy up?*

Do a detailed feedback session on these things and plan how you will change, cut or add things to the show and make those little changes.

Exercise 33 – Tell us our story

Ask someone to watch the show and take notes on the story. Ask them to tell you what the story is back when you are done.

Does this match what you thought it was?

It's a nice way of simply hearing what someone got from the whole. It may surprise you!

Exercise 34 – Repeat

After this, I want you to run the final version of the show three times before you do the final performance of it. This is so it's completely in your bodies and minds. Practice makes perfect. Make tiny changes but nothing major; this is much more about committing things to memory at this stage.

Now you are ready to do your show!

GOOD LUCK, it is going to be AMAZING, babes xx